Franz Rosenthal

A Grammar of Biblical Aramaic

PORTA LINGUARUM ORIENTALIUM
Neue Serie
Herausgegeben von Werner Diem und Franz Rosenthal

Band 5

1995
Harrassowitz Verlag · Wiesbaden

Franz Rosenthal

# A GRAMMAR OF BIBLICAL ARAMAIC

Sixth, revised edition

1995

Harrassowitz Verlag · Wiesbaden

Photo on the cover courtesy ISRAEL ANTIQUITIES AUTHORITY
(4Q Dan[b] containing D 6:8–21).

Die Deutsche Bibliothek – CIP-Einheitsaufnahme
Ein Titeldatensatz für diese Publikation ist bei Der Deutschen Bibliothek erhältlich

Die Deutsche Bibliothek – CIP Cataloguing-in-Publication-Data
A catalogue record for this publication is available from Die Deutsche Bibliothek

e-mail: cip@dbf.ddb.de


Gedruckt auf alterungsbeständigem Papier.
Druck und Bindung: Hubert & Co., Göttingen
Printed in Germany

ISSN 0554-7342
ISBN 3-447-03590-0

## Table of Contents

## Preface

The purpose of this grammar is twofold. It is, on the one hand, to provide the beginner with the elements of the language, and, on the other, to prepare him—surreptitiously as it were—for possible research in the problems of Aramaeology. These two aims may seem mutually contradictory, and it must be admitted that they are to a degree. However, the attempt is always worth making, and Biblical Aramaic, representing the comparative simplicity of the old consonant writing with the complexities of a much later stage of the spoken language superimposed upon it, is a strenuous training ground.

Biblical Aramaic grammars are customarily written in the assumption that the reader will have previously acquired a good knowledge of Biblical Hebrew. This assumption may be correct, but it seems a poor justification for not giving Biblical Aramaic its due as a language in its own right. Therefore, no knowledge of Hebrew is presupposed here. Brevity has made it necessary to deal lightly with many of the Masoretic refinements, and no lengthy discussions of Semitic peculiarities, let alone comparative excursuses, were possible. But the presentation, it is hoped, will be clear for the student with or without much grounding in other Semitic languages.

Knowledge of the syntax is important in any language, and in Aramaic where the syntax in particular reflects the history of the language most faithfully, it is of crucial significance. I have taken cognizance of this fact by *not* writing a special discussion of Biblical Aramaic syntax, since I know that few beginning students of a language ever take the trouble of reading the portion of the grammar dealing with syntax. Instead, the most important syntactic notions have been added to appropriate passages of the grammatical treatment. This often involves anticipating linguistic points not yet discussed, but I believe that the reader will not find this unduly disturbing.

The basis of this grammar is the text as published in the "Kittel Bible," that is, the third edition of the *Biblia Hebraica*

(Stuttgart, 1937), originally organized by R. Kittel. The text of Ezra was prepared by H. H. Schaeder, and that of Daniel by W. Baumgartner. Subsequent editions—I have before me one labeled the ninth being a reproduction of the seventh (Stuttgart, 1954)—contain no changes in the Aramaic portions. As this is the most authoritative text presently available, it is imperative here to follow it to the letter. Even details of orthography and vocalization are nearly always accepted as they appear in the *Biblia Hebraica*. However, it should be realized that manuscript variations as far as orthography and vocalization are concerned are numerous and important, and the text of the *Biblia Hebraica* does not constitute the last word with regard to them. Moreover, while the work of the Masoretes is most remarkable for its linguistic accuracy and reliability, most of the progress in our understanding of the contents and the languages of the Bible depends on our increasing ability of going beyond it.

Very little, if anything, that is new will be found in this grammar. There exist some good grammars by outstanding scholars and one recent, excellent dictionary. However, there should be room for one more attempt to help students to acquire a basic preparation in a language that holds the key to a good deal of the world's intellectual history, and I am extremely grateful to the publisher and the editors of the *Porta* that they have given me the opportunity to make this attempt. I also had the good fortune of being able to draw upon the knowledge of several outstanding authorities. First among them was H. L. Ginsberg with whom I was privileged to discuss my manuscript and who made many substantial contributions. A further reading of the manuscript by F. M. Cross proved most helpful and yielded valuable suggestions. A reading of the proofs by M. Pope contributed important corrections and improvements. The section on Akkadian loan words (par. 188) has greatly benefitted from the advice of A. Goetze, and the section on Persian loan words (par. 189f.) and the Persian etymologies in the glossary were revised by W. B. Henning who thus did for this grammar what F. C. Andreas did many years ago for its predecessor in the *Porta*.

* * *

Few abbreviations have been used. They are either self-evident or have been explained in the proper places. An asterisk is used to indicate forms or form elements not attested in Biblical Aramaic; two asterisks occasionally indicate that the form-elements so marked are not known from other Official Aramaic texts either, but they have not been used consistently. No asterisks have been used in connection with the paradigms. In transliterations, primary and secondary word stress is indicated by _́ and _̀, respectively (par. 28). An arbitrary sign ≤ has been chosen to indicate penult stress in Aramaic writing (par. 26).

* *
*

The preceding preface was written for the first edition which appeared in 1961. As stated in brief remarks to the second through fifth printings, only very minor changes and additions to the bibliography were made in them. For the second printing, I acknowledged my indebtedness to observations communicated to me by M. Pope and Rabbi T. Gluck as well as to reviews by H. L. Ginsberg (in *Journal of Biblical Literature*, LXXX [1961], 386 f.) and H. Michaud (in *Syria*, XXXVIII [1961], 327 ff.).

"An Index to the Biblical Passages cited in Franz Rosenthal, *A Grammar of Biblical Aramaic*" was published by G. R. Wilson, in *Journal of Semitic Studies*, XXIV (1979), 21–24. It has been included in the French translation of this *Grammar* that was made by Paul Hébert and published in a series entitled *Sessions de langues bibliques* directed by Jean Margain (Paris 1988).

The present edition has been revised with some care and great restraint. Attention has been paid to the enormous scholarly output of the last two decades in the field of Aramaic in general as well as Biblical Aramaic. The resulting conflict between conciseness, which I feel is the main virtue of my work, and completeness has been resolved in favor of the former. Interesting and useful as a discussion of the new ideas proposed might have been, it would have distracted from clarity and directness. It is well known that progress in scholarship consists of the creation of new problems. This is as true for revisions in the vocabulary as it is for major theories. A more profiled outline of dialectal distinctions within pre-Christian Aramaic inside and outside the

Official Aramaic matrix is slowly emerging, with consequences for Biblical Aramaic, but it still is sketchy and dim. And owing to the linguistic concern with spoken languages and the happy circumstance that in the Semitic languages including Aramaic a wealth of spoken dialects has become readily accessible, we have now at our disposal new materials for insights into phonology and syntax whose proper understanding for the student of a language is obvious. All this will eventually have a certain impact also on Biblical Aramaic grammar.

The "Kittel Bible" continues here as the basis for the grammatical presentation, regardless of any new material that may have become available for its text. It has meanwhile appeared in a new recension under the official title of *Biblica Hebraica Stuttgartensis*. I have before me the second edition dated in 1984. Ezra and Nehemiah were edited for it by Wilhelm Rudolph, Daniel remained assigned to W. Baumgartner. The text as such remains unchanged. Changes are by and large restricted to the critical apparatus and the Massora. The vocalization of the Leningrad manuscript (L) has been followed even in dubious cases where it was disregarded in the earlier Kittel Bible. See, for instance, D 2:8 (*-ṯọ̄n* for *-ṯūn*); D 2:10 אֱנָשׁ for -אֱ; the appearance of the doubling dot in *ṭ* and *m* in D 3:10 טְעֵם (cf. 4:25) and D 7:4 דִּי־מְרִיטוּ; *ẹ̄* for *ī* in D 3:15 דִּי. D 4:27 reads בִּתְקַף, with no reference to קְ as attested in the Kittel Bible and elsewhere (see Additions and Corrections to par. 10, below). In D 2:35, the normal הֲוָת is restored without comment (see par. 145).

More material for the Aramaic text has now become available from Qumrān (Ulrich, Bibliography [b]) and will have to be evaluated grammatically. This, however, cannot, and should not, be done here.

* *
*

The following Additions and Corrections are marked in the margin of the text by numbers corresponding to those indicated on pp. 5—8. The very few passages where minor changes have been made in the text itself have remained unmarked..

1 par. 6 (p. 12):

The final forms of .... The forms used in the beginning and within words ....

2 par. 8 (p. 12):

The use of internal vowel letters is now attested with greater frequency in the Ancient Aramaic period, cf., in particular, Muraoka (Bibliography [a]) who assumes Akkadian influences. However, the view that it originated with final long vowels has not yet been refuted.

3 par. 10 (p. 15):

In a similar phrase, the Qumran text of Enoch has *tqwp*, as against the more frequent spelling *tqp*, see Fitzmyer-Harrington (Bibliography [a]), no. 18 : 3. This is, of course, not absolutely decisive for the BA form. It could still have been pronounced with an *a* vowel as related forms listed in par. 51 under *pu*$^{c}$*l* (if their *a* vowels do indeed represent the norm). A long *ā* here is out of the question. For another problem caused by the same alternation, see Additions and Corrections to par. 52, below.

4 par. 12 (p. 16):

For a recent attempt to locate the historical place for Massoretic *k*$^{ə}$*t̲īb-q*$^{ə}$*rē̤*, see Fassberg and Morrow (Bibliography [c]).

5 par. 15 (p. 17):

For a much more complicated, and probably more correct picture of the process of spirantization, cf. Kaufman, *Akkadian Influences*, 16f., and idem, in *Journal of the American Oriental Society*, CIV (1984), 87—95.

6 par. 18 (p. 20):

Kaufman, *Akkadian Influences*, 112, doubts that *zāk̲ū* is a loan from Akkadian and prefers Canaanite influence.

7 par. 31 (p. 24) and par. 49 (p. 30):

The form *-kn* appears in Hermopolis papyrus no. V attached to the masc. sg. and pl. noun. Use of the masc. form for the fem. seems rather less likely.

8 par. 51 (p. 31):

See above, to par. 10. For *ktwl*, see Fitzmyer-Harrison, no. 7:4, but outside a meaningful context.

9 par. 52 (p. 32):

*zmn* appears with short *a* in D 7:12 and with long *ā* in D 2:16. The coexistence of *zaman* and *zamān* is attested in Arabic but remains enigmatic in view of the unsolved problem of the word's etymology. The suffixed forms give no indication of an original long *ā*, and a confusion in the BA vocalization appears to be the preferable assumption.

10 par. 93 (p. 44):

The particle *ṣd'* without *h* is found in Qumran, Targum of Job 34:12 (Fitzmyer-Harrington, 5, 34:6, p. 30). This shows that *hṣd'* was analysed already in ancient times as composed of the interrogative particle plus *ṣd'*, whether this is correct or not.

11 par. 99 (p. 46), par. 130 (p. 53), par. 166 (p. 57), and par. 188 (p. 62):

Whether puʿʿal should have an asterik or not depends on the interpretation of *mswblyn*. Now that the root *sbl* "to carry" is more frequently attested, scholars seem more inclined to see in *mswblyn* a puʿʿal formation of it (*mᵊsobbᵊlīn*), perhaps meaning something like "supported." The matter is far from being settled.

12 par. 99 (p. 46):

In Qumrān, *'ṯ-* is more frequent than *hiṯ-*.

13 par. 145 (p. 55):

See the remarks (above, p. 4) on the Stuttgart Bible.

14 par. 157 (p. 56):

Kaufman, *Akkadian Influences*, 104, thinks of *škll* as rather an old inherited word, and not necessarily a borrowing from Akkadian.

15 par. 178 (p. 60):

Kaufman, *op. cit.*, 55, suggests Akk. *ḫāṭu* in the sense of "to examine" for יַחִיטוּ, as the Akk. word does occur in connection with *temennu* "foundation."

16 par. 188 (pp. 61 f.):

Doubts about the specifically Akkadian origin of some of these loanwords have been expressed by Kaufman, *op. cit.* Note, in particular, that *parsu* is not attested as a monetary unit. On the other hand, Kaufman sees Akkadian influence on BA words such as *אֵב from *inbu*; *ša-la* as a prototype of דִּי לָא; אֻשַּׁיָּא from *uššu*; זְקִיף as influenced by *zaqīpu* (?); שָׁלֵה, שָׁלוּ as related to *šillatu* "blasphemy, audacity," which is widely accepted. See also the Addenda and Corrigenda above, to paragraphs 18, 99, 157, 178.

17 Bibliography:

The first publication of the *Comprehensive Aramaic Lexicon* project (*CAL*) appeared in the beginning 1992. It is entitled *An Aramaic Bibliography. Part I: Old, Official, and Biblical Aramaic*, by J.A. Fitzmyer and S.A. Kaufman, with the collaboration of S.F. Bennett and E.M. Cook (Baltimore 1992). It is of immense usefulness, but the small and highly selective Bibliography here may still serve as a good introduction for the student of BA. The choice has been difficult, and the weeding process has been aimed at saving space and says nothing about quality, especially as regards the omission of some older items.

18 Glossary:

Numerous glossaries are appearing in rapid succession, but it does not seem invidious to single out two of them. H.L. Ginsberg (in Rosenthal [ed.], *An Aramaic Handbook*, I,2, 16—41), being finetuned to explaining the text, adds occasional grammatical and syntactical information, emendations of the text, and more precise English equivalents. K. Beyer, *Die aramäischen Texte*, 503—741, places the BA vocabulary in a wider Aramaic context, thereby possibly obscuring dialectical boundaries but providing for a better understanding of BA lexicography and grammar. *CAL* can be expected to fulfill this purpose on a much larger scale.

A few minor corrections have been made in the text. Add further:

19 p. 85 (גְּלָל):

The most recent of the many attempts to find a precise meaning for אֶבֶן גְּלָל is that of Williamson (Bibliography [d]): "especially selected stone" (such as stone used for sculpture and the like).

20 pp. 88 and 100 (חוט, חיט, יחט):

See above, to par. 178.

21 p. 89 (חרץ*):

See Wolters (Bibliography [d]) who translates D 5: 6 not implausibly: "losing sphincter control."

22 p. 96 (סובל):

See above, to par. 99.

23 p. 100 (רגשׁ):

The precise meaning remains very much in doubt.

24 p. 102 (שָׁלֵה, שָׁלוּ):

See above, to par. 188.

25 p. 102 (שְׁמִין*):

The vocalization שְׁמַיִן would seem preferable.

## I. The Texts and the Language

1. Aramaic passages occur in the Old Testament in four places:

Ezra 4:8—6:18 and 7:12—26 (documents from the Achaemenid period concerning the restoration of the temple in Jerusalem).

Daniel 2:4—7:28 (five Oriental historical tales involving Jews and an apocalyptic vision).

Jer. 10:11 (a stray Aramaic sentence in a Hebrew context denouncing idolatry).

Gen. 31:47 (two words translating a Hebrew toponym into Aramaic said to be the language of Laban).

Certain Hebrew texts of the Bible have been recognized as translations from an Aramaic original.

2. The native name of the language was Aramaic. This is indicated by the (Hebrew) gloss *ʾ$^a$rāmīṯ* E 4:7, D 2:4, introducing Aramaic passages in about the same manner in which Aramaic papyri from Egypt use, for instance, *mṣryt* to indicate use of an Egyptian term.

3. The Aramaic texts of the Bible come from periods separated, approximately, by as much as three centuries. They represent different types of literature. They were written by men belonging to different strata of society. And, in all likelihood, they originated in different localities. Yet, the language they use appears to all intents and purposes uniform, with only minor divergences. This strange fact is explained by the history of Aramaic.

The earliest Aramaic inscriptions discovered so far come from the ninth century B. C. At the beginning of our era, Aramaic, in various dialectal forms, was the dominant spoken language of Syria and Mesopotamia. It developed a number of literary dialects, known as Palestinian Jewish Aramaic, Samaritan, and Syro-Palestinian Christian Aramaic along the Eastern border of the Mediterranean, and Syriac, Babylonian Talmudic Aramaic, and Mandaic in Mesopotamia. To this day, there are small groups that speak Aramaic dialects, such as the inhabitants of some villages in the Anti-Lebanon, Christians and Jews living in or originating from

Azerbaijan and Kurdistan, to which may be added remnants of the gnostic sect of the Mandaeans, familiar with the tradition of their dialect.

During the second millennium B. C., various Aramaic dialects are likely to have been spoken at the borders and within Mesopotamia and the Fertile Crescent. But it was the dialect used by Aramaeans settled within the confines of Assyria that from the eighth century on supplanted all other Aramaic dialects. According to 2 Kings 18:26, Aramaic was, at the end of that century, an international language understood by high Assyrian and Jewish officials but not by the common people of Jerusalem. When the Achaemenids conquered Mesopotamia in the second half of the sixth century and established their vast empire, they continued the use of Aramaic as the medium for written communication in their far-flung administration. By that time, Aramaic was the dominant spoken language in Mesopotamia. It was making steady headway as a spoken language in the lands of the Fertile Crescent, including Palestine.

The use of this "Official Aramaic" of the Achaemenid Empire outlasted the latter's existence by some centuries. Official Aramaic, when written by people whose native language was not Aramaic, showed considerable divergences in a number of aspects, especially in the syntax and the vocabulary. When it was used by native speakers of Aramaic, local dialectal differences made themselves felt. At first, these were inconspicuous, but they grew more and more pronounced with the political and religious fragmentation of the Aramaic speaking area, and eventually made their appearance as distinct dialects.

The Aramaic of the Bible as written has preserved the Official Aramaic character. This is what makes it nearly uniform in linguistic appearance. It also makes it largely identical with the language used in other Official Aramaic texts. Most numerous among these are the Aramaic documents of the Achaemenid period discovered in Egypt which are invaluable for the understanding of Biblical Aramaic (henceforth abbreviated BA).

## II. The Writing

**4.** The letters of the BA alphabet are the same as are used in Hebrew. The so-called Hebrew or square script is, in fact, a Jewish specialization of the older Official Aramaic script adopted by the

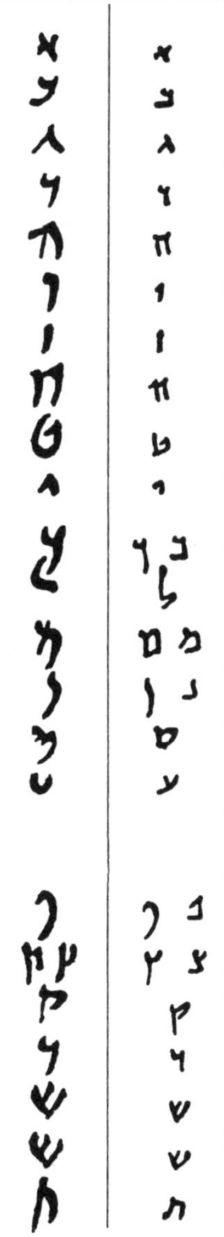

| | Egypt 5th cent. B.C. | Dead Sea Scrolls (Qumrān) 1st cent. B.C. to 1st cent. A.D. | Transliteration | Name | Approximate Pronunciation |
|---|---|---|---|---|---|
| א | | | ʾ | ʾālep̄ | glottal stop |
| ב | | | b, ḇ | bẹ̄ṯ | b, spirant b (bilabial v) |
| ג | | | g, ḡ | gimel | g, spirant g |
| ד | | | d, ḏ | dāleṯ | d, spirant d (like *th* in *there*) |
| ה | | | h | hẹ̄ | h |
| ו | | | w | wāw | w |
| ז | | | z | zayin | z |
| ח | | | ḥ | ḥẹ̄ṯ | pharyngal fricative h |
| ט | | | ṭ | ṭẹ̄ṯ | "emphatic" (i.e., velarized) t |
| י | | | y | yọ̄ḏ | y |
| כ (ך) | | | k, ḵ | kap̄ | k, spirant k |
| ל | | | l | lāmeḏ | l |
| מ (ם) | | | m | mẹ̄m | m |
| נ (ן) | | | n | nūn | n |
| ס | | | s | sāmeḵ | s |
| ע | | | ʿ | ʿayin | voiced laryngal (similar to the sound of incipient vomiting) |
| פ (ף) | | | p, p̄ | pẹ̄ | p, spirant p (bilabial f) |
| צ (ץ) | | | ṣ | ṣāḏẹ̄ | "emphatic" s |
| ק | | | q | qọ̄p̄ | "emphatic" k |
| ר | | | r | rẹ̄š | r |
| שׂ | | | ś | śīn | palatalized (?) s |
| שׁ | | | š | šīn | sh |
| ת | | | t, ṯ | tāw | t, spirant t (like *th* in *think*) |

Jews in the course of their acceptance of Official Aramaic and the increasing use of Aramaic as a spoken language among them.

The writing runs from right to left.

The forms of the letters in brackets are those occurring at the end of a word.

The names of the letters are those commonly used in Hebrew grammar.

**5.** אהוי may be used as vowel letters (par. 10). א and ה are used for final *ā* or *ẹ̄*, ו for *ū* or *ọ̄*, and י for *ī* and *ẹ̄*. Final *ē*, which occurs very rarely, is indicated by ה.

א appears as vowel letter in connection with final *ọ̄* in לְגוֹא "into" and the proper name עִדּוֹא. This use is frequent in later Jewish Aramaic documents and appears to have resulted from the spelling of (Hebrew) לֹא (לוֹא) "not." Note that the Dead Sea (Qumrān) fragment of D 3:24 has לוֹ, although the spelling וא- for final *ọ̄* is common in the Dead Sea documents. Cf., further, par. 13.

*1* **6.** The final forms כנפצ are the earlier forms of these letters. The forms used within words represent a later development. The closed form of final ם, on the other hand, is derived from the older open מ. The consistent distinction between final and non-final letters appears to be not earlier than the third century B. C.

In the Egyptian documents and the Dead Sea material, words are separated from each other by a clearly noticeable blank space. Exceptions are rare. The same situation no doubt prevailed when the BA texts were committed to writing.

**7.** Consonant doubling (par. 20) is indicated by a dot placed in the geminated letter.

A dot is also used to indicate non-spirantized pronunciation of בגדכפת (par. 15).

It occurs further in connection with final ה in order to indicate that it is not used as a vowel letter but is to be pronounced as a consonant.

*2* **8.** Ancient Aramaic developed an incomplete system of indicating vowels by using certain consonants (par. 5). This started with final long vowels but was soon extended to internal long vowels (except *ā*). The Biblical text shows a more systematic but still far from consistent application of this kind of vocalization (par. 10, 13).

The use of special vowel signs for the Biblical text is of a much later date. It is in general not earlier than the seventh century A. D. The men who provided the Biblical texts with vowels signs are known as Masoretes ("transmitters"). Their efforts began with occasional indications of some vowels but developed into systems meant to be a complete (and rather complicated) phonetic notation.

There are three vowel systems known, the Palestinian, the Babylonian, and the Tiberian. The one in use in our Bible texts is the Tiberian. There are many small differences in vocalization within the various manuscripts and systems of vocalization.

The systems of vocalization were invented primarily for the Hebrew text. Influence of Hebrew phonetic peculiarities upon the vocalization of BA may be assumed on occasion. However, since the phonetic habits of the Masoretes were formed by Aramaic speech, their systems of vocalization may be assumed rather to represent Aramaic speech habits.

The Tiberian system favors the Palestinian pronunciation of Aramaic. The Babylonian system leans toward that of Mesopotamia; notwithstanding its importance, little attention has perforce been paid to it in this grammar. BA texts with Palestinian vocalization are not available.

In the Tiberian system, the vowel sign is placed underneath the letter that is followed by the vowel in question. An exception is the vowel ọ̄ which is placed on top and to the left of the letter.

Final vowelless חהע, after a long vowel other than *ā*, are furnished with an *a* vowel placed a little to the right, indicating a preceding ultra-short $^{a}$ that is heard when the consonants in question are pronounced correctly (-$^{a}$*ḥ*, -$^{a}$*ʿ*; there is no example for -*h*).

In the Babylonian (and Palestinian) systems, the vowel signs are placed on top of the consonants.

**9.** The vowel signs do not indicate vowel quantity (length or brevity) but vowel quality. For a proper understanding of the attempt made in the following paragraph to distinguish between long and short vowels, it will be well to keep in mind that the Semitic languages know extremely stable long vowels used to indicate certain basic noun and verb formations. All the other vowels are exceedingly unstable and run the gamut from ultra-shortness to what at times may strike the listener as almost a long vowel. The Masoretes aspired to catching and noting down the finest vowel shades such as were due to the influence of surrounding consonants, word and sentence stress, etc. This is a very difficult task that can be successfully accomplished only for a living language under carefully controlled conditions. How far the subtle Masoretic distinctions are applicable to the pre-Masoretic period of BA remains doubtful.

**10.** These are the Tiberian vowel signs:

◌ְ indicates vowellessness. Final vowelless consonants have no such sign, with the exception of ךְ and תְּ.

Since vowellessness in BA is very frequently the result of the disappearance of short vowels, it may not always have been complete but a murmured vowel may have remained, especially where otherwise there would have appeared consonant clusters that were hard to pronounce. In such cases, we cannot decide whether there was vowellessness or a murmured vowel. The sign ᵊ has been used for transliterating them.

The sign ◌ְ may be combined with one of the following three vowel signs in order to indicate ultra-short vowels: ◌ֲ ᵃ; ◌ֳ ᵒ; ◌ֱ ᵉ. These are used in connection with אהחע instead of simple ◌ְ, whenever it is in the place of an original vowel. But they may also occur in positions where there was no vowel originally (לֶהֱוֵא "he will be," לְהַחֲוָיָה "to inform," אָחֳרָן "another," מַעֲבָדוֹהִי "His works").

They may also be used following or preceding ק and ג, or preceding לנר: קֳדָם "before," לָקֳבֵל "corresponding to," קֱרִי "it was read" E 4:18, 23, מַדֱּקָה, מַדֲּקָה "crushing" D 7:7, 19, גֱּלִי, גְּלִי "it was revealed" D 2:19, 30, סֲגַר "he locked" D 6:23, מְמַלֱּלָה "speaking" D 7:11, בֱּנַיְתַהּ "I built it" D 4:27, צִפֲּרֵי "birds" D 4:9.

◌ַ *a* (short).

◌ָ *ā*. Original long *ā* must have been pronounced by the Masoretes like long open *o*, since its short form is *o* (short) in the following cases:

(1) in closed unstressed syllables: כָּרְסֵא "chair," דָּכְרָנַיָּא (*doḵrānayyā*) "memoranda," פָּלְחָן (*polḥān*) "cult," כָּל קֳבֵל (*kol qᵒḇẹl*) "corresponding to."

(2) when followed by ֳ, or by ָ in a closed unstressed syllable: לָקֳבֵל (loqᵒḇel), הָחָרְבַת (hoḥorḇaṯ) "was destroyed."

(3) when it represents ֳ under secondary stress in the preposition קֳדָם "before": קָדָמַי (qòḏāmáy) "before me," but קֳדָמֵיהוֹן (qᵒḏàmẹ̄họ̄n) "before them."

(4) possibly in תְּקָף "strength" D 4:27. 3

ֶ *e* (open, short). In אֵ֫לֶּה "these," it may possibly represent a long vowel. For עֲלֶ֫ינָא, cf. par. 49, and for נִדְנֶה, cf. par. 190.

*e* is very close to *a*, cf., for instance, יְדְהֹם "their hand" E 5:8, for *יְדֵהֹם, or אֶחָיךְ "your brothers (colleagues)," for אַחַיךְ (par. 62). The Babylonian system has no sign for it but uses *a*. However, *e* also occurs as a variant of *ẹ/i* (יִפֵּל, but יִפֶּל לָךְ *yippellā́ḵ*, par. 118).

ֵ *ẹ*, *ẹ̄* (closed). Most frequently, ֵ represents short *ẹ*, as in בְּעֵל "master," הוֹתֵב "he settled," etc., also in cases where it alternates with *i* (יִתְעֲבֵד, יִתְעֲבִד "will be made").

Secondary lengthening may have been operative in some of these cases. Lengthening may also be assumed where ֵ appears in unstressed open syllables (par. 23): עֵטָה "counsel," לְחֵנָתֵהּ "his maids," גֵּוָה "arrogance," יְקֵדַת "burning." This, however, is not certain since ֵ in בְּטֵלַת (*bᵊṭẹlā́ṯ*) "was idle" E 4:24, is certainly short.

ֵ represents a long vowel at the ends of words when it is followed by one of the vowel letters אהי; or, within words, when it is followed by the vowel letter י; or where it represents the result of the sound change *ẹ/iʾ* > *ẹ̄* (לְמֵאמַר "to say," לְמֵזֵא "to heat," בֵּאדַ֫יִן "then," etc.).

ִ *i*, *ī*. Long *ī* is as a rule followed by the vowel letter י. There are exceptions such as מְדִנָן "provinces" E 4:15, כְּפִ֫תוּ "they were fettered" D 3:21, שַׁלִּטִן "mighty" (pl. masc.) D 4:23, זִוַי "my splendor, splendid looks" D 4:33. The more remarkable use of י where short *i* is required appears in מַשְׁפִּיל "bringing down" D 5:19, הַלְבִּ֫ישׁוּ "they dressed" D 5:29, קְרִ֫יבוּ "they drew near" D 6:13, שֵׁיזִיב "he saved" D 6:28.

ֹ *ọ*, *ọ̄* (closed), as a long vowel usually combined with the vowel letter ו (וֹ), but occasionally occurring without it, in particular after *-w* (*-wọ̄*). It may appear in stressed syllables which when they are not stressed would exhibit short *o* or *u*: קְשֹׁט "truth," כֹּל "all," גֹּב (גּוֹב D 6:13) "den." In these cases, a short but closed *ọ*, rather than a long vowel, may be intended. Short *ọ* in כֻּלָּא (*kọ́llā*) "totality," גֹּדּוּ (*gọ́ddū*) "cut down!" (pl. masc.) D 4:11, אֹרְחָתֵהּ "His ways."

ֻ *u*, *ū*, as a long vowel usually expressed by the sign וּ, but cf. לְבֻשֵׁיהוֹן "their garments" D 3:21, לְהוֹדָעֻתַנִי "to let me know" D 2:26, etc. In תְּהוֹדְעוּנַּנִי "you let me know" D 2:5 and similar forms, *ū* may have been shortened in pronunciation but retained as a historical spelling; ו appears in these cases in the Aramaic documents from Egypt, whereas BA spelling vacillates between וּ und ֻ (par. 175).

**11.** The signs of the Babylonian system are: ⁻ for vowellessness; *a*, *e*; *ā*; *ẹ*, *ẹ̄*; *i*, *ī*; *ọ*, *ọ̄*; *u*, *ū*.

4 **12.** *Kᵊṯīḇ—Qᵊrẹ̄*: In a number of cases, according to the Masoretes, words "written" (*kᵊṯīḇ*) in one way are to be "read" (*qᵊrẹ̄*) in another. Some of these are of considerable grammatical importance, as, for instance, אַנְתְּה (*ántā*, read *ant*) "you" (sg. masc.), דָּאְרִין (*dāʾᵃrīn*, read *dāyᵊrīn*) "dwelling" (part. pl. masc.), נְפַלוּ (*nᵊp̄álū*, read *nᵊp̄álā*) "they (fem.) fell" (where the *kᵊṯīḇ* may, in fact, be a corruption of *נְפַלִי), etc.

The often expressed *a priori* assumption that the consonant text (*kᵊṯīḇ*) represents the more original form of the text is, as far as BA is concerned, a dangerous oversimplification.

## III. Remarks on Phonology

**13.** In addition to its use as a vowel letter at the ends of words (par. 5), א also occurs as a silent letter:

(1) in words where it became silent and was retained as a historical spelling: רֵאשׁ (< *riʾš*-) "head," מָאנַיָּא (< *maʾnayyā*) "vessels," מֹאזַנְיָא (= מֹאזְנַיָּה, < *mawzan*-, spelled with א as in Hebrew) "scales" D 5:27, בָּאתַר (< *baʾᵃṯar*) "after" but בָּתְרָךְ D 2:39, מָאתַיִן (< *maʾt*- < *miʾat*-) "two hundred," דָּנִיֵּאל „Daniel," הוּא (*hū* < *huʾa*) "he," הִיא (*hī* < *hiʾa*) "she." The origin of the א in צַוְּארֵהּ (*ṣawwᵊrẹh*) "his neck" D 5:7 (as in Hebrew spelling) is not clear.

(2) in particular grammatical forms where it became silent: יֵאמַר (< *yiʾmar*) "he says," לְמֵאמַר (< *miʾmar*) "to say," but phonetic spellings are also found (מֵמַר, לְמֵתֵא "to come," לְמֵזֵא "to heat"); לֵאלָהָיךְ (< *leʾ-*) "to your gods," בֵּאדַיִן (< *beʾ-*) "then."

(3) in final vowelless position, or after a zero or murmured vowel: שַׂגִּיא (*śaggī*), but שַׂגִּיאָן (*śaggīʾān*) "much, many," בִּאישְׁתָּא (*bīštā*) "evil" E 4:12, but בְּאֵשׁ "was bad" D 6:15, מָרִאי (*mārī*) "my lord," but שָׂנְאָיךְ (*śānᵊʾāḵ*) "your enemies" D 4:16.

(4) in the distorted pronunciation of foreign proper names: בֵּלְטְשַׁאצַּר (< **Balāṭ-šarri-uṣur*?), בֵּלְשַׁאצַּר, בֵּלְאשַׁצַּר (< *Bēl-šar-uṣur*).

**14.** א results occasionally from *-āy-*, as in כַּשְׂדָּיאָ (*Kaśdāʾā* < *Kaśdāyā*) "Chaldaean," תְּלִיתָיאָ (*tᵊlīṯaʾā* < *tᵊlīṯāyā*) "third" (fem.), קָאֵם (*qāʾem* < *qāyem*) "standing." Inversely, we find חֲטָיָךְ (*ḥᵃṭāyāḵ*) "your sins" D 4:24 for *חֲטָאָךְ (*ḥᵃṭāʾāḵ*).

**15.** Spirantization of בגדכפת ("*bᵊḡaḏkᵊp̄aṯ*") is an Aramaic devel- 5
opment which, in all likelihood, was under way in the sixth century B. C. It takes place after vowels and after zero or murmured vowels resulting from the disappearance of an original vowel. This includes forms such as מַלְכִין (< *malaḵīn*) "kings," כִּדְבָה (< *kaḏaḇā*) "untrue" (fem.).

The ת of the fem. ending shows *t* rather than *ṯ* in בִּאישְׁתָּא (*bīštā*) "evil" E 4:12, מְדִינְתָּא (*mᵊḏīntā*) "province" E 5:8, 6:2, עֲבִידְתָּא (*ʿᵃḇīḏtā*) "work" E 5:8, D 2:49, מָרָדְתָּא "rebellious" E 4:12, but בִּירְתָא "fortress" E 6:2. Spirantization is always found after *ē*: חֵיוְתָא "animal," שְׁאֵלְתָא "question," אֵימְתָנִי "frightful." Note the spirantization of ג in the Persian loan word פִּתְגָם "message, word."

Spirantization also takes place after the diphthong *-ay-*: בַּיְתָא "house," הַיְתִי "he brought."

**16.** Within the sentence, בגדכפת (at the beginning of a word following a word ending in a vowel) are spirantized when the words in question are thought to be closely connected. In practice, such close connection is indicated by a short line connecting the letters at the top (for instance, דִּי־דְהַב), or by the use of a connecting "accent." The "accents," which are either "dividing" or "connecting," are special signs placed on top or underneath each word, usually but not always on the syllable receiving primary stress. Connecting accents requiring spirantization that occur in BA are:

ַ (but *not* | ַ), ֑ (placed *after* the vowel sign), ֖, ֔ (but *not* ֔ placed upon the last consonant of the word), ֒ (placed upon the last consonant of the word), and ֖.

Occasional exceptions are admitted: בְּבָבֶל ַ "in Babylon" E 5:17, כְּחָכְמַת ֖ (unstresssed) "like the wisdom of" D 5:11, in each case because of the sequence of three identical or similar consonants; דְּתָבְרַיָּא ַ "law officials" D 3:2, דְּתָבְרַיָּא ֒ D 3:3; פְּסַנְתֵּרִין ֑ "psaltery" D 3:5, but פְּסַנְתֵּרִין ַ D 3:10 (this being a case much discussed by the Masoretes who appear to have been undecided how to fit the Greek letter into Aramaic speech habits).

As a rule, it is easy to see why in a given case close connection requiring spirantization is assumed, but no fixed rules can be given. The negation always requires spirantization for the following word. Demonstrative pronouns beginning with ד also show spirantization in connection with nouns to which they belong, an exception being, however, רָזָה דְנָה "this secret" D 2:18.

**17.** BA ח corresponds to two different phonemes of the original Semitic stock of consonants (*ḥ* and *ḫ* [*kh*]).

BA דטת each correspond to two, ע to three different phonemes of the original Semitic stock of consonants. ד corresponds to *d* and *ḏ*, ת to *t* and *ṯ*, ט to *ṭ* and *ṱ* (*ḏ̣*, *ẓ*), and ע to *ʿ*, *ḍ*, and *ġ*:

| Semitic | Ugaritic | Hebrew | Aramaic | Arabic |
|---|---|---|---|---|
| d | d | ד | ד | د |
| ḏ | d | ז | ד | ذ |
| z | z | ז | ז | ز |
| t | t | ת | ת | ت |
| ṯ | ṯ | שׁ | ת | ث |
| š | š | שׁ | שׁ | س |
| ṭ | ṭ | ט | ט | ط |
| ṱ (ḏ̣, ẓ) | ṱ (ḏ̣) | צ | ט | ظ |
| ṣ | ṣ | צ | צ | ص |
| ʿ | ʿ | ע | ע | ع |
| ḍ | ṣ | צ | ע (ק) | ض |
| ġ | ġ | ע | ע | غ |

Examples:

*d*: יְדַע "he knew," יַד "hand."

*ḏ*: דִּכְרָן (Hebrew זִכָּרוֹן) "memorandum," דְּבַח (Hebrew זָבַח) "he sacrificed," מַדְבְּחָא "altar," דְּהַב (Hebrew זָהָב) "gold," אֶדְרָע (Hebrew זְרוֹעַ) "arm," the demonstrative element ד in the pronouns דִּי, דָּא, דְּנָה, and the adverb אֱדַיִן, etc. Note that this sound was originally spelled with ז in Official Aramaic. An original ז sound in a Persian loan word (גִּזַּבְרַיָּא "treasurers" E 7:21) was wrongly spelled with ד in D 3:2f. (גְּדָבְרַיָּא).

*z*: זָיְעִין (זאעין) "trembling," מָזוֹן "food."

*t*: בַּיְתָא "house," כְּתַב "he wrote," מַתְּנָן "gifts."

*ṯ*: תַּמָּה (Hebrew שָׁם) "there," תְּלָת (Hebrew שָׁלוֹשׁ) "three," תּוֹר (Hebrew שׁוֹר) "ox," תְּרַע (Hebrew שַׁעַר, < *ṯaġr*) "door," יְתִב (Hebrew יָשַׁב) "he sat."

*š*: רֵאשׁ "head," שְׁמַיָּא "heaven," שְׁאֵל "he asked," שְׁמַע "he heard."

*ṭ*: טָב "good," טַבָּחַיָּא "butchers, executioners," שַׁלִּיט "mighty," טַל "dew."

*ṯ̣*: קַיִט (Hebrew קַיִץ) "summer," תַּטְלֵל (Hebrew צֵל) "seek shade (shelter)," עֵטָא, יָעֲטֹהִי (Hebrew יעץ) "advice, his advisers," טִפְרוֹהִי, טִפְרַיהּ (Hebrew צִפֹּרֶן) "his (its) nails," טוּר (Hebrew צוּר) "mountain," נִטְרֵת (Hebrew נצר) "I guarded."

*ṣ*: צָבֵא "wishing," צֶלֶם "image," הַצְלַח "prospered," קַצִּצוּ "cut down!" (pl. masc.).

*ʿ*: עֲבִידְתָּא "work," עַם "people," יְדַע "he knew," בְּעֵל "master."

*ḍ*: אַרְעָא (Hebrew אֶרֶץ) "earth," עֲמַר (Hebrew צֶמֶר) "wool," עִלְעִין (Hebrew צֵלָע) "ribs," עָרָךְ (Hebrew צַר, צֹרֵר) "your enemies," אָע (< עע, Hebrew עֵץ) "wood," יְמַחֵא (< מחע, Hebrew מחץ) "he hits (stays His hand)," רְעוּת (Hebrew רצה) "wish." In an older stage of Aramaic, Semitic *ḍ* was represented by a sound which was distinct from ע and written ק. This ק is preserved in BA as a historical spelling only in אַרְקָא Jer. 10:11, along with מֵאַרְעָא in the same verse.

*ġ*: עַל "he entered," בְּעָא "he desired, requested."

**18.** Seeming exceptions to these rules require an explanation. Thus, שָׁפְטִין "judges" E 7:25 should be *תפטין; consequently, it cannot be Aramaic but is a loan word from the Canaanite-Hebrew
6 family. זָכוּ "innocence" must be a legal loan word from the Akkadian, because the original root was *ḏkw*. Likewise, (א)שֵׁיצִי "he completed" E 6:15 must be an Akkadian loan word if only because the Aramaic development of the original root (*wḏʾ*, Aramaic *yqʾ*, *yʿʾ*) has ע.

**19.** שׂ became ס in later Aramaic. In BA times, this process was in its incipient stages. שׂ, in Aramaic words, is as a rule used correctly. Exceptions are סַתְרֵהּ "he tore it down" E 5:12 and, possibly, יִסְבַּר "he intends" D 7:25. Vacillation between שׂ and ס occurs in foreign words, and although this is due to uncertainty concerning the foreign sound, it foreshadows the Aramaic sound change *ś* > *s*: אַרְתַּחְשַׁשְׂתְּא "Artaxerxes" E 4:8, etc., but אַרְתַּחְשַׁסְתְּא E 7:21, כַּשְׂדָּי in D, but כַּסְדָּיאָ "Chaldaean" E 5:12, שַׂבְּכָא "sambuke (harp)" D 3:10, 15, but סַבְּכָא D 3:5, שְׁרֹשִׁי (< שְׂרֹשִׁי, *kᵉtīḇ* שרשו) "corporal punishment" E 7:26, corresponding to סרושיתא occurring in an Aramaic leather document from Egypt.

**20.** Consonant doubling in BA involves true gemination; the doubled consonant is pronounced twice with a syllable break in between. Final consonants are not doubled (cf. גֻּבָּא — גֹּב "den," עַמָּא — עַם "people," פֻּמַּהּ — פֻּם "mouth").

All consonants are capable of gemination except א and ר. The dot indicating gemination is also not used with החע. This suggests that at certain times and in certain areas, החע were also not capable of gemination. But forms with nasalization (הַנְעֵל for *haʿʿel*) or preceding short vowel (הַ֫עֵלְנִי *haʿʿélnī* "let me enter" D 2:24f.) confirm the existence of gemination for these consonants.

Short vowels before א and ר are lengthened. In the case of א, the only instance is מֵאַרְעָא "from the earth" Jer. 10:11. For ר, cf., for instance, מְבָרַךְ (< *mᵉḇarrak̲*) "blessed," תָּרָעַיָּא (< *tarrāʿayyā*) "doorkeepers." Vowel lengthening is also occasionally found before ע, cf. מְרָעַע (< *mᵉraʿʿaʿ*) "breaking" D 2:40, מְסָעֲדִין (< *mᵉsaʿʿᵃḏīn*) "helping" (pl. masc.) E 5:2. The only instance of lengthening before ה: מִתְבָּהַל "disturbed" D 5:9 is doubtful, and gemination, as usual in the case of החע, seems preferable.

**21.** Substitution of nasalization for gemination is frequently found: תִּנְדַּע (< *tiddaʿ*) "you will know" E 4:15, מַנְדַּע (< *maddaʿ*)

"knowledge," לְהַנְסָקָה "to bring up," next to הֻסַּק "he was brought up," D 6:24.

Where original *n* appears unassimilated, secondary nasalization, instead of retention of the original sound, may be involved.

**22.** Original long vowels have been retained throughout. This applies also to *ā*, which became *ọ̄* in Hebrew at an early period: טָב (Hebrew טוֹב) "good," תְּלָת (Hebrew שָׁלוֹשׁ) "three."

אֱנוֹשָׁא (*ʾᵃnọ̄šā*, read *ʾᵃnāšā*, the common form) "mankind" is not a Hebraism, but originated through vowel assimilation from **ʾunāš* (cf. תְּחוֹת **tuḥāt* "underneath"). The suffixed element *-ọ̄n* is found in noun formations in addition to *-ān*: דִּכְרוֹנָה E 6:2 and דָּכְרָנַיָּא "memorandum," שִׁלְטֹנֵי "officials" D 3:2f., and שָׁלְטָן "rule," רַעְיוֹנַי (in Bab. vocalization *riʿyọ̄n-*) "my thoughts." עֶלְיוֹנִין "most high," on the other hand, is a Hebraism (par. 187). -מְדוֹר and -מְדָר "dwelling" are different noun formations.

**23.** Short vowels in unstressed open syllables have been reduced to a zero or murmured vowel. Inversely, preservation of a short vowel in an open syllable usually requires that that syllable be stressed. Cf., for instance, תְּלָת (*tᵊlāṯ* < *ṯalāṯ*, Hebrew שָׁלוֹשׁ with pretone lengthening) "three," כְּתַבוּ (*kᵊṯáḇū* < *katabū*, Hebrew כָּתְבוּ *kā̀ṯᵊḇū́*) "they wrote," סְלִקוּ (*sᵊlíqū* < *saliqū*) "they went up." For בְּטֵלַת, cf. par. 10.

In some cases, short *a* was retained in pronunciation and became lengthened secondarily: מְרִים "raising up" D 5:19, יְהָקֵים "he sets up" D 5:21, 6:16 (par. 141). Cf. also מָזוֹן "food."

Note the strange absence of the gemination of מ in חַרְטֻמַיָּא "magicians" D 4:4, 6, and אֻמַיָּא "nations" D 3:4 (but אֻמַּיָּא E 4:10).

**24.** Short *i/ẹ* before החער closing a syllable becomes *a*: אָמַר "saying" (but שָׁאֵל "asking"), מְשַׁבַּח "praising" (but מְמַלִּל "speaking"). In verbs ending in החער, this process extends to open syllables (par. 115).

**25.** Occasional pausal lengthening of short vowels is admitted in Tiberian vocalization: חָיִל "strength" E 4:23, D 3:4, יְדָי "my hands" D 3:15, קֳדָמָי (< *qᵒḏāmay*) "before me" D 2:6, שָׁמְרָיִן (< *Šåmᵊráyin*) "Samaria" E 4:10, 17, עֲנָיִן (< *ʿᵃnáyin*) "humble, poor" D 4:24.

**26.** The main word stress falls usually on the last syllable.

Penult stress occurs in certain grammatical formations where the suffixed element has a long vowel. This applies to:

(1) independent personal pronouns (par. 29): אֲנַ֫חְנָה "we" (but *ʾªná*, *himmọ́*).

(2) pronominal suffixes (par. 31): הַעֲ֫לְנִי "let me enter!" אֲבֿ֫וּהִי "his father," הַקְרְבֿ֫וּהִי "they brought him near," עֲל֫וֹהִי "upon him," אֲבָהָ֫תַנָא "our fathers," etc. However, the suffix of the 1. sg. in connection with nouns and prepositions is always stressed, except in אֲ֫בִי "my father" D 5:13.

(3) suffixed elements of the verb: יְדַ֫עְתְּ "you knew," כְּתַ֫בוּ "they wrote," שְׁאֵ֫לְנָא "we asked," אֱכֻ֫לִי "eat!" (sg. fem.), שְׁבֻ֫קוּ "leave!" (pl. masc.), יֵאבַ֫דוּ "let them perish!" (par. 108), etc. Exceptions are the endings of verbs originally having אוי as their last consonant wherever these endings result from contraction (-ọ́ < -*áyū*, etc., par. 145ff.).

(4) the adverbial ending -*ā* (par. 88), including אָסְפַּ֫רְנָא (*ʾospárnā*) "exactly," כֹּ֫לָּא (*kọ́llā*) "totally."

Penult stress further occurs where the vowel of the last syllable merely serves the purpose of dissolving a consonant cluster: אֶ֫בֶן (< *ʾabn*) "stone," קַ֫יִט "summer," and equivalent noun formations (par. 51); יְדַ֫יִן "hands" and other duals (par. 45); הַשְׁכַּ֫חַת "I found," סָ֫פַת "it (fem.) ceased," and similar verbal forms (par. 117). Also דָּרְיָ֫וֶשׁ (*Dārᵊyáweš*) "Darius," כּ֫וֹרֶשׁ "Cyrus," but בָּבֶל (*Bāḇél*) "Babylon."

Exceptional cases of penult stress are כְּנֵ֫מָא "thus," מֶ֫נִּי "appoint!" (par. 153), אֵ֫לֶּה "these" (par. 32).

**27.** Enclitic use of the prepositions ל and ב, or of a genitive, may deprive a word of its stress or result in an exceptional stress (principal or secondary) on the penult: וְיֵאמַר לֵהּ (*wᵊyẹ́marlẹh*) "and says to Him" D 4:32, הוּסְפַת לִי (*hūsᵊpaṯlí*) "was given to me in addition" D 4:33, מִתְעֲבֵד בַּהּ (*miṯʿªḇeḏbáh*) "being done in it" E 4:19, גִּבָּרֵי חַיִל (*gibbàrẹ̄-ḥáyil*) "strongmen" D 3:20, בִּסְפַר דָּכְרָנַיָּא (*bìsᵊpar-doḵrà-nayyá*) "in the record book" E 4:15.

**28.** Secondary stress occurs in words of more than two syllables. In the Biblical text, it is often indicated by a short vertical line to the left of the vowel sign (ָֽ, ָֽ, etc.). Where this line occurs to the right of the vowel sign (ָֽ), it was added by the editors of the "Kittel Bible" but is not found in the manuscripts.

In transliteration, ◌́ indicates the main stress, ◌̀ the secondary stress.

## IV. The Pronoun

**29.** Independent personal pronouns:

| | sg. | | pl. |
|---|---|---|---|
| I | אֲנָה | we | אֲנַ֫חְנָה |
| you (masc.) | אַנְתְּ, אַנְתָּה (ʾántā, *read* ʾant) | you (masc.) | אַנְתֻּם*, אַנְתּוּן |
| you (fem.) | אַ֫נְתִּי* | you (fem.) | אַנְתֵּן** |
| he | הוּא | they (masc.) | הִמּוֹ, הִמּוֹן, אִנּוּן |
| she | הִיא | they (fem.) | אִנִּין |

The spelling אֲנַ֫חְנָא is found in E 5:11, אַנְתְּ in E 7:25.

הִמּוֹ occurs in E, הִמּוֹן in D. With one exception (אֲנַ֫חְנָא הִמּוֹ עַבְדוֹהִי "we are His servants" E 5:11), both הִמּוֹ and הִמּוֹן happen to be used as direct objects immediately following a verb in the perfect tense.

**30.** The pronouns of the third person may be used as the copula, even where the subject of the sentence is a pronoun of the first or second person: דִּי הוּא אֱלָהָא חַיָּא "who is the living God" D 6:27, דִּי הִיא שְׁנַת "which is the year . . ." E 6:15, חֲדָה הִיא דָתְכוֹן "one (and the same) is the law applicable to you" D 2:9, הֲלָא דָא הִיא בָּבֶל "is this not Babylon?" D 4:27, דִּי אִנִּין אַרְבַּע "which are four" D 7:17, אֲנַ֫חְנָא הִמּוֹ עַבְדוֹהִי "we are His servants" E 5:11, אַנְתְּה הוּא רֵאשָׁה דִּי דַהֲבָא "you are the head of gold" D 2:38, אַנְתְּה הוּא דָנִיֵּאל "you are Daniel?" D 5:13, מַן אִנּוּן שְׁמָהָת גֻּבְרַיָּא "what (par. 38) are the names of the men?" E 5:4. The only example of an indetermined predicate is וּמַן הוּא אֱלָהּ דִּי "and who is *a* god who . . ." D 3:15.

**31.** Pronominal suffixes: In addition to the independent personal pronouns, BA has pronominal suffixes that may be added to nouns (par. 49, cf. also par. 95), prepositions (par. 77ff.), and verbs (par. 174ff.). In connection with nouns, these suffixes represent possessive pronouns, and in connection with prepositions and verbs, the objective case of the independent personal pronoun.

The basic forms are:

| | sg. | pl. |
|---|---|---|
| 1. | ־ִי (־נִי with verbs) | ־נָא |
| 2. masc. | ־ָךְ | ־כֹם, ־כוֹן |
| 2. fem. | ־כִי* | ־כֵן* |
| 3. masc. | ־הּ (-*ẹh*), ־הִי (after long vowels) | ־הֹם, ־הוֹן |
| 3. fem. | ־הּ (-*ah*) | ־הֵן (*kᵊṯīḇ* ־הֵון) |

The 3. pl. suffix is not used with verbs (cf. par. 174).

An independent objective pronoun, formed by *יָת with suffix, occurs in BA only once: יָתְהוֹן "them" D 3:12.

An independent possessive pronoun is formed by the relative pronoun דִּי followed by the preposition לְ: חָכְמְתָא וּגְבוּרְתָא דִּי לֵהּ הִיא "wisdom and power are His" D 2:20.

**32.** Demonstrative pronouns:

| | sg. | | pl. |
|---|---|---|---|
| masc. | דְּנָה | masc./fem. | אִלֵּין (אֵלֶּה, אֵלֶּה) |
| fem. | דָּא | | |
| masc. | דֵּךְ | | אִלֵּךְ |
| fem. | דָּךְ | | |
| masc. | דִּכֵּן | | |
| fem. | דִּכֵּן | | |
| masc. | הוּא | | אִנּוּן |

אֵלֶּה (*ʾẹllē*) occurs in Jer. 10:11, אֵלה (read *ʾẹl*) in E 5:15.

אִלֵּךְ occurs only as masc., but the fem. can be assumed to be identical in form.

For הוא and אִנּוּן (independent personal pronouns used as demonstrative pronouns), cf. הוּא צַלְמָא "that image" D 2:32 and מַלְכַיָּא אִנּוּן "those kings" D 2:44.

After prepositions, BA knows a demonstrative element ה that is assimilated to the pronominal suffixes (par. 89).

**33.** The demonstrative pronoun can be used as a noun: עַל דְּנָה "concerning this," כִּדְנָה ,לָקֳבֵל דְּנָה "in accordance with this, thus," דְּנָה הוּא "this is it" D 2:28, דָּא לְדָא "the one . . . the other" D 5:6, דָּא מִן דָּא "the one from the other" D 7:3. Cf., in particular, the use of the masc. with reference to a fem. noun: מִלָּה כִדְנָה "a matter like this" D 2:10.

**34.** Used as an adjective, the demonstrative pronoun usually follows the noun to which it belongs. This noun must have the definite article or an equivalent form of determination, i. e., it must be in the construct state (par. 48), or have a pronominal suffix, or be a proper name.

Cases of demonstrative pronouns preceding the noun are: דְּנָה בִנְיָנָא "this building" E 5:4, אֵלֶּה מָאנַיָּא "these vessels" E 5:15, הוּא צַלְמָא "that image" D 2:32, דְּנָה חֶלְמָא "this dream" D 4:15, אִלֵּין חֵיוָתָא "these animals" D 7:17.

**35.** The relative pronoun is דִּי. It is used for all genders and numbers.

The form דְּ (< דִּי), which is common in later Aramaic, occurs in the misreading דֶּהָוֵא (*Dehhāyẹ*) E 4:9, for דְּהוּא "that is".

For further uses of דִּי, cf. par. 86.

**36.** As דִּי cannot be declined, oblique cases must be indicated by pronominal suffixes attached to appropriate components of the relative clause. Cf. אַנְתָּה ... דִּי אֱלָהּ שְׁמַיָּא ... יְהַב לָךְ "you ... to whom the God of Heaven gave" D 2:37, דִּי כָל מַעֲבָדוֹהִי קְשֹׁט "all of whose works are as they should be" D 4:34, דִּי מַלְכָּא שָׂם שְׁמֵהּ בֵּלְטְשַׁאצַּר "whose name the king had made Belteshazzar" D 5:12, דִּי נִשְׁמְתָךְ בִּידֵהּ "in Whose hand your soul is" D 5:23.

The direct object case, however, is only rarely indicated in this or any other manner. Examples for the direct object relationship expressed by a pronominal suffix are: דִּי פֶחָה שָׂמֵהּ "whom he had made governor" E 5:14, דִּי אֲנָה בֱנַיְתַהּ לְבֵית מַלְכוּ "which I have built for a royal capital" D 4:27, דִּי אַנְתְּה פָּלַח לֵהּ "whom (par. 182) you worship" D 6:17, 21.

**37.** The indefinite relative pronouns are:

מַן דִּי "whoever"
מָה, מָה דִּי "whatever."

Simple דִּי "whatever (whomever)" is found in D 5:19.

**38.** The interrogative pronouns are:

מַן "who?"
מָה "what?"

The use of מַן in E 5:4, מַן אִנּוּן שְׁמָהָת גֻּבְרַיָּא "what(!) are the names of the men?", reflects the thought: "who are the men?".

## V. The Noun and the Adjective

**39.** Nouns and adjectives, unless they are of non-Semitic origin, may be classified as belonging to "roots" composed of two or, in most cases, three consonants (or "radicals"). They may be further classified according to modifications that the root may undergo through (1) the use of various short or long vowels following the radicals, (2) the gemination of the second or third consonant, or (3) the addition of prefixed (ʾ-, *m*-, *t*-) or suffixed (*-ān*, *-ọn*, *-iṯ*, *-ūṯ*, *-āy*) elements. Instead of gemination of the second or third consonant, one also finds reduplication of a two-consonant root (הַרְהֹרִין "imaginings") or of the last two consonants of a three-consonant root (שְׁפַרְפָּרָא "dawn"). In BA, all words of four or more consonants are of foreign origin either as recent loan words or as ancient cultural terms (as, for instance, פַּרְזֶל "iron").

As a convenient mode of reference, grammarians have chosen one particular root, such as *pʿl* (*qṭl*, *ktb*), to indicate a given nominal or adjectival formation, for instance, *paʿl*, *pᵊʿāl*, *mip̄ʿal*, *pᵊʿalʿāl*, etc. *Ktb* has the advantage of indicating *bgdkpt* spirantization.

**40.** Some nominal and adjectival formations have come to be associated with certain categories of meaning. Thus, *pᵊʿīl* and *paʿʿīl* are widely used for adjectives (דְּחִיל "frightful," שַׁלִּיט "mighty," חַכִּים "wise"). *Paʿʿāl* is used to indicate professional status (דַּיָּנִין "judges," טַבָּחַיָּא "butchers, executioners," זַמָּרַיָּא "musicians," תָּרָעַיָּא "doorkeepers"), and so is *pā'ōl*, represented by כָּרוֹזָא "herald." The preformative *ma-*, *mi-* often indicates locality (*מִשְׁתְּיָא "place where one drinks, banquet"). The suffixes *-īṯ*, *-ūṯ* (par. 56f.) have come to denote abstract meaning (מַלְכָּא "king," מַלְכוּתָא "kingship, kingdom"). The "gentilic" ending *-āy* (par. 58) indicates belonging to something.

**41.** Nouns have two genders, masc. and fem.; three numbers, sg., pl., and dual; and three "states," corresponding to the form without the definite article ("absolute state" = *abs. st.*), the form used before a depending noun that is in the position of our genitive ("construct state" = *cstr. st.*), and the form with the definite article ("determined state" = *det. st.*).

There is no formal distinction between nouns and adjectives. Adjectives are placed after the nouns to which they belong and to which they conform grammatically as closely as possible.

**42.** Nouns and adjectives are declined as follows:

| | masc. sg. | fem. sg. |
|---|---|---|
| abs. st. | טָב "good" | טָבָה |
| cstr. st. | טָב | טָבַת |
| det. st. | טָבָא | טָבְתָא |
| | **masc. pl.** | **fem. pl.** |
| abs. st. | טָבִין | טָבָן |
| cstr. st. | טָבֵי | טָבָת |
| det. st. | טָבַיָּא (יְהוּדָיֵא) | טָבָתָא |

Formations with the gentilic ending *-āy* (par. 58) have *-ē*, instead of *-ayyā*, in the det. st. of the pl. masc.

The original spelling of the postpositive article is א-, but instances of a spelling with ה- occur, in particular in connection with the sg. masc.

The original spelling of the ending of the abs. st. fem. is ה-, but sporadic examples of spellings with א- occur.

For irregular non-spirantization of the ending of the det. st. of the sg. fem., cf. above, par. 15.

־ִים, instead of ־ִין, as the ending of the abs. st. of the pl. masc. (מַלְכִים "kings" E 4:13, אֲנָשִׁים "men" D 4:14, אַלְפִים "thousands" D 7:10), is a Hebraism.

**43.** The definite article is a demonstrative element. Therefore, it can also serve to indicate the vocative: מַלְכָּא לְעָלְמִין חֱיִי "O king, live for ever!" For the ending *-ā* as a remnant of an ancient accusative, cf. par. 88.

**44.** The fem. is used to form nouns from adjectives: שְׁחִיתָה "corruption" D 6:5, עַמִּיקָתָא וּמְסַתְּרָתָא "deep and hidden matters" D 2:22, חַשְׁחָן "needed things" E 6:9, רַבְרְבָן "big words" D 7:8.

**45.** The dual is preserved only in remnants. It is used with parts of the body that occur in pairs in nature: יְדַיִן "hands", רַגְלַיִן "feet," שִׁנַּיִן "two (rows of) teeth" D 7:7. In such nouns, the dual may be used for the pl.: קַרְנַיִן עֲשַׂר "ten horns" D 7:7. Further duals are מָאתַיִן "two hundred" and תְּרֵי (cstr. st. masc.), תַּרְתֵּין (fem.) "two."

All other forms of the dual of the masc. noun, including those with pronominal suffixes, are identical with the pl. forms and not distinguishable from them. No dual of a fem. formation or of an adjective is found.

**46.** Use of the abs. st. and the det. st. agrees by and large with the non-use or use of the definite article in English. The det. st. may also be used for the general designation of species: חַמְרָא שָׁתֵה "he was drinking *wine*" D 5:1, מָאנַיָּא דִּי בֵית אֱלָהָא דִּי דַהֲבָה וְכַסְפָּא "the vessels of *gold* and *silver* belonging to the house of God" E 5:14.

The numeral חד "one" is used occasionally to denote indetermination in the sg.: אִגְּרָה חֲדָה "a letter" E 4:8, מְגִלָּה חֲדָה "a scroll" E 6:2, צְלֵם חַד "an image" D 2:31, שָׁעָה חֲדָה "an hour (a while)" D 4:16, אֶבֶן חֲדָה "a stone" D 6:18, שְׂטַר חַד "one side" D 7:5.

Note in the following enumeration how the nouns of Greek origin, in contrast to the Aramaic ones, are left without the definite article: קָל קַרְנָא מַשְׁרוֹקִיתָא קַיתְרוֹס סַבְּכָא פְּסַנְתֵּרִין סוּמְפֹּנְיָה וְכֹל זְנֵי זְמָרָא "the sound of the horn, pipe, *zither*, sambuke (harp), *psaltery*, *symphony* (bagpipe?), and all kinds of music(al instruments)" D 3:5, 7, 10, 15.

47. The cstr. st. implies determination: מִלַּת מַלְכָּא "*the* word of the king."

Indetermination of the first element of a genitive construction must be expressed by some sort of circumlocution: מֶלֶךְ לְיִשְׂרָאֵל רַב "*a* great king of Israel" E 5:11.

We call the second element "genitive" because it is found in positions where Semitic and Indo-European languages that have preserved case endings use the genitive. If this genitive is in the abs. st., the entire construction may seemingly be indetermined, as in עֲנָשׁ נִכְסִין "a property fine" E 7:26, בַּר אֱלָהִין "a divine being" D 3:25.

The cstr. st. may be used before a prepositional expression: מַלְכְוָת תְּחוֹת כָּל שְׁמַיָּא "the kingdoms underneath the entire heaven" D 7:27. But, in general, nothing can come between a cstr. st. and its depending genitive. Thus, demonstrative pronouns referring to the noun in the cstr. st. follow at the end: בֵּית אֱלָהָא דְנָה "this house of God".

It is possible for more than one genitive to depend upon a single noun in the cstr. st.: מִלֵּי מַלְכָּא וְרַבְרְבָנוֹהִי "the words of the king and his magnates" D 5:10, etc.

48. The cstr. st. is the basic form for expression of the genitive relationship. However, there are altogether three different ways to express a genitive construction in BA:

| | | |
|---|---|---|
| (a) | בֵּית אֱלָהָא | "the house of God" |
| (b) | בַּיְתָא דִּי אֱלָהָא | |
| (c) | בַּיְתֵהּ דִּי אֱלָהָא | |
| (a) | שְׁמָהָת גֻּבְרַיָּא | "the names of the men" |
| (b) | שְׁמָהָתָא דִּי גֻּבְרַיָּא | |
| (c) | שְׁמָהָתְהֹן דִּי גֻּבְרַיָּא | |

The use of the cstr. st. is preponderant in BA. Construction (c), with proleptic pronominal suffix, is comparatively rare. The intermediate form (b) appears to have come into use originally in order to break up long strings of successive genitives but in BA, it is used indiscriminately alongside the cstr. st. Cf., for instance, עֲבִידְתָּא דִּי מְדִינַת בָּבֶל "the administration of the Province of Babylon" D 2:49, but עֲבִידַת מְדִינַת בָּבֶל D 3:12, גֹּב אַרְיָוָתָא "the lions' den" D 6:8, 13, 25, but גֻּבָּא דִּי אַרְיָוָתָא D 6:17, 20.

**49.** The noun with pronominal suffixes:

| masc. sg. | | fem. sg. | |
|---|---|---|---|
| אֱלָהִי | "my god" | חֵיוְתִי | "my animal" |
| אֱלָהָךְ | "your" (masc.) | חֵיוְתָךְ | |
| אֱלָהֵכִי* | "your" (fem.) | חֵיוְתֵכִי* | |
| אֱלָהֵהּ | "his" | חֵיוְתֵהּ | |
| אֱלָהַהּ | "her" | חֵיוְתַהּ* | |
| אֱלָהָנָא | "our" | חֵיוְתָנָא* | |
| אֱלָהֲכֹם (-כוֹן) | "your" (masc.) | חֵיַוְתְכֹם (-כוֹן)* | |
| אֱלָהֲכֵן* | "your" (fem.) | חֵיַוְתְכֵן** | |
| אֱלָהֲהֹם (-הוֹן) | "their" (masc.) | חֵיַוְתְהֹם (-הוֹן)* | |
| אֱלָהֲהֵן | "their" (fem.) | חֵיַוְתְהֵן** | |

| masc. pl. | | fem. pl. | |
|---|---|---|---|
| אֱלָהַי | "my gods" | חֵיוָתִי | "my animals" |
| אֱלָהָיךְ | "your" (masc.) | חֵיוָתָךְ | |
| אֱלָהֵיכִי* | "your" (fem.) | חֵיוָתֵכִי* | |
| אֱלָהוֹהִי | "his" | חֵיוָתֵהּ | |
| אֱלָהַיהּ | "her" | חֵיוָתַהּ | |
| אֱלָהַינָא | "our" | חֵיוָתַנָא | |
| אֱלָהֵיכֹם (-כוֹן) | "your" (masc.) | חֵיוָתְכֹם (-כוֹן)* | |
| אֱלָהֵיכֵן* | "your" (fem.) | חֵיוָתְכֵן** | |
| אֱלָהֵיהֹם (-הוֹן) | "their" (masc.) | חֵיוָתְהֹם (-הוֹן) | |
| אֱלָהֵיהֵן | "their" (fem.) | חֵיוָתְהֵן** | |

Note the *kᵊtīḇ-qᵊrē̦* distinction in the pl. of the masc. noun: אֱלָהָיךְ (*ʾᵉlāhāḵ*), אֱלָהַיהּ (*ʾᵉlāhah*), אֱלָהַינָא (*ʾᵉlāhánā*).

The vowel preceding the suffix of the 1. pl. is variously given. Thus, we find אֱלָהָנָא "our god" D 3:17, אֲבָהָתַנָא "our fathers" E 5:12, לְשֵׁיזָבוּתַנָא "to save us" D 3:17, אִיתַינָא "we are" D 3:18, לַנָא "for us" E 4:14, עֲלֶינָא "to us" E 4:12, 18, 5:17. The evidence strongly favors short stressed *a* (> *e* in *ʿᵃlénā*).

The suffix of the 3. pl. fem. is written like the corresponding masc. form: כָּלְהֵון "all of them" D 7:19, בֵּינֵיהֵון "between them" D 7:8.

**50.** Wherever the final consonant of the root is preceded by a long vowel, no changes in the vocalization of the word are required by the declension or by the addition of the pronominal suffixes.

In other noun formations, minor changes in the vocalization may result, among which the following may be noted:

**51.** *Paʿl, piʿl, puʿl* (and corresponding fem. forms): The abs. and cstr. st. of the masc. becomes *pᵊʿa/ẹ/ọl.*

For original *paʿl*, cf. כְּסַף "silver," אֲלַף "thousand," תְּלַג "snow," חֲמַר "wine," גְּבַר "man" (pl. גֻּבְרִין, Bab. vocalization *gabrīn*), טְעֵם "order," צְלֵם "image," עֲבֵד "slave," בְּעֵל "master." In לְחֶם "meal, banquet" D 5:1, the unusual *e* (ms. variant reading with *ẹ*) may represent *a*. Whenever an ending is added, we find the original form: כַּסְפָּא, אַלְפָּא, טַעְמָא, מַלְכְּתָא "queen," etc., but also שִׁמְשָׁא "sun."

For original *piʿl*, cf. פְּשַׁר "interpretation," סְפַר "book," מְלַח "salt." With endings, we find פִּשְׁרָא, סִפְרִין, מִלְכִּי "my advice," חֶלְמָא "dream," גֶּשְׁמְהוֹן "their body," בִּקְעַת "plain" (cstr. st.).

For original *puʿl*, cf. קְשֹׁט "truth," כְּתַל "wall" D 5:5 (pl. כֻּתְלַיָּא E 5:8), and, presumably, רְגַז "wrath" and תְּקֹף (*tᵊqop̄*, Bab. vocali- 8
zation *tᵊqọp̄*, par. 10) "strength." With endings, *o* is the preferred vowel: תָּקְפָּא "strength", נָגְהָא "dawn," שָׁרְשׁוֹהִי "its roots," עָפְיֵהּ "its foliage," חָכְמָה, חָכְמְתָא "wisdom," אֹרְחָתֵהּ "His ways," but כֻּתְלַיָּא "the walls."

However, these noun formations have another abs. and cstr. st. with anaptyctic vowel after the second consonant (*péʿel, pẹ́ʿel* [*páʿal*, on account of the laryngal]). This is the accepted form in Hebrew. Cf. מֶ֫לֶךְ "king," קֶ֫רֶן "horn," צֶ֫לֶם "image," אֶ֫לֶף "thousand," חֱ֫לֶם "dream," טְ֫עֵם "order," and, in a loan word, פַּרְשֶׁ֫גֶן "copy."

The original pl. formation of *pa/i/uʿl* was **pa/i/uʿalīn*, with an *a* vowel in the second syllable. This vowel has left a trace in the preserved spirantization of following בגדכפת: מַלְכִין "kings," עַבְדּ֫וֹהִי "his slaves," but נִסְכֵּיהוֹן "their libations" E 7:17. יַרְכָתֵהּ "its thighs" may be rather a *paʿil* formation.

In roots with *y* as the second consonant, we always find the form with the anaptyctic vowel in the abs. st.: קַ֫יִט "summer," חַ֫יִל "strength." In the cstr. st., the original diphthong is contracted: בֵּית "house," חֵיל "army," עֵין "eye." In all other forms, the diphthong is preserved; in D 4:1, the variant reading בַּיְתִי, "my house" is preferable to the accepted form בֵּיתִי.

**52.** Word formations with two short vowels (*paʿal*, etc.). Their declension is governed by the rule of the disappearance of short unstressed vowels in open syllables (par. 23): דְּהַב, דַּהֲבָא (with *ḇ*) "gold," אֲתַר, אַתְרֵהּ "place," חַבְרוֹהִי "his companions," בְּשַׂר, בִּשְׂרָא
9 "flesh, mankind," זְמַן, זִמְנָא "time." The *i* vowel in the last two cases is secondary ($a > i$).

**53.** Word formations with a long and a short vowel are also governed by the same rule: אָשַׁף, אָשְׁפִין "enchanter," עָלַם, עָלְמִין "eternity."

**54.** Words ending in *-y*, such as *פְּתָי, פְּתָיֵהּ "its breadth," show no irregularities.

חֲדוֹהִי "its breast," מְעוֹהִי "its belly" D 2:32 appear to belong to *חֲדֵה, *מְעֵה, forming a dual/plural *חֲדַיִן, *מְעַיִן (cf. the participles בְּנֵה, בְּנַיִן, par. 150). However, a number of words ending in *-y*, such as כָּרְסֵא (*korsẹ̄*) "chair," אַרְיֵה "lion," לֵילְיָא "night" (det. st.), with suffix כָּרְסְיֵהּ "his chair," have the pl. כָּרְסָוָן, *כָּרְסָוָת, כָּרְסָוָתָא, אַרְיָוָתָא.
מָרֵא "lord, master" presupposes a form where final א has become *y* (det. st. *מָרְיָא), rather than an original *mārīʾ*. However, "my lord" is מָרִאי ($m\bar{a}r\bar{\imath} < m\bar{a}r^{\partial}{}^{\flat}\bar{\imath}$).

**55.** In word formations of roots with final *w*, *w* is retained in the one masc. formation *חזו, חֶזְוָא "vision." In fem. formations, there are three possibilities: (1) *w* may be retained as in חֶדְוָה "joy." (2) It may become *ọ̄*, as in חֱזוֹתֵהּ "its appearance." But (3) in most cases, it becomes *ū*, as in רְבוּ "greatness," צְבוּ "(some)-thing," שָׁלוּ "neglect," בָּעוּ "request," cstr. st. רְעוּת "wish," with the definite article or pronominal suffixes רְבוּתָא, רְבוּתָךְ, גָּלוּתָא "exile," בָּעוּתֵהּ. This formation has become indistinguishable from the abstract ending *-ūṯ*. In fact, in some of these words, the original root ended in *y*, and the preponderance of *ū* is due to the influence of the abstract ending.

**56.** Nouns with the abstract ending *-ūṯ*: Abs. st. מַלְכוּ "kingdom," בְּהִילוּ "haste," נַהִירוּ "brilliance," שָׂכְלְתָנוּ "intelligence." Cstr. st. מַלְכוּת, חַשְׁחוּת "needs." Det. st. מַלְכוּתָא, שָׂהֲדוּתָא "testimony." With suffix מַלְכוּתִי.

The pl. is *מַלְכְוָן, מַלְכְוָת, מַלְכְוָתָא.

57. The endings -ī, -īṯ: Long -ī serves as a fem. ending in אֵימְתָנִי (-ān-ī) "frightful." In אָחֳרִי (ʾoḥ°rī) "other" (fem. of אָחֳרָן), it may go back to an original ending -ay > -ẹ̄.

The abstract ending has the abs. st. -ī, cstr. st. -īṯ, det. st. -īṯā, pl. *-ᵊyān, etc. It is sparsely represented: שְׁרֹשִׁי (kᵊṯīḇ שרשו) "corporal punishment" E 7:26 (where the ending y belonged to the original Persian word but was interpreted as the Aramaic formative, cf. par. 19, 189), אַחֲרִית "end" D 2:28, אַרְעִית "bottom" D 6:25, מַשְׁרוֹקִיתָא "pipe" D 3:5, 7, 10, 15, עִלִּיתֵהּ "its upper room" D 6:11; נְוָלִי "dunghill" D 2:5, 3:29 (but נְוָלוּ E 6:11) is of uncertain origin and formation (par. 190) but seems to have been adapted to this class of nouns.

58. The ending -āy (gentilic formations and ordinal numbers): The det. st. of the pl. ends in -ẹ̄, cf. יְהוּדָיֵא "Jews," בָּבְלָיֵא "Babylonians," כַּשְׂדָּיֵא (Kaśdāʾẹ̄) "Chaldaeans."

Between the ā and another vowel, y is frequently replaced by the glottal stop (par. 14), which occasionally appears also expressed in writing: כַּשְׂדָּאִין D 3:8, יְהוּדָאִין (Yᵊhūḏāʾīn, read Yᵊhūḏāyīn!) D 3:12.

In certain foreign words, such as אֲפַרְסַתְכָיֵא "magistrates" (?) E 4:9, תִּפְתָּיֵא "police chiefs," addition of the ending -āy seems erroneous in view of their meaning and origin.

59. Nouns without the fem. ending may nevertheless be fem. in gender. Such nouns are parts of the body that occur in pairs: יַד "hand," *רְגַל "foot," *עַיִן "eye," קֶרֶן "horn," שִׁנַּיִן . . . רַבְרְבָן "two big (rows of) teeth" D 7:7. Other parts of the body that are fem. in gender are תְּלָת עִלְעִין "three ribs" D 7:5, גַּפִּין אַרְבַּע "four wings" D 7:6 (but masc. D 7:4). *אֶצְבַּע "finger" has the fem. pl. ending, אֶצְבְּעָן.

Further fem. nouns are אֶבֶן "stone," *אֲרַע "earth," *צִפַּר "bird" (D 4:18, but in D 4:9, the kᵊṯīḇ of the verb, יְדֻרוּן צִפֲּרֵי שְׁמַיָּא "the birds of heaven dwell," is masc.), דָּת (a Persian loan word where the final t may have suggested the fem. gender). Others, such as עִזִּין "(she) goats," are fem., though the grammatical gender is not apparent in BA.

רוּחַ "spirit, wind" is usually fem., but masc. in D 2:35. Likewise, נוּר "fire," fem. in D 3:6, etc., is used as masc. in D 3:27, 7:9. Cf. also רֵיחַ נוּר לָא עֲדָת "the smell of fire did not come forth" D 3:27, where the fem. form of the verb may refer to "fire" rather than "smell"; a Dead Sea (Qumrān) variant reads the masc. עדה.

Names of cities and countries may be fem.: בָּבֶל רַבְּתָא "Babylon the great" D 4:27.

**60.** Masc. sg. formations may have the ending of the fem. pl. Cf. par. 54 and 62, also אֶצְבְּעָן (fem.) "fingers" and אֹרְחָתֵהּ (presumably fem.) "His ways."

**61.** Fem. sg. formations taking the masc. ending in the pl. are מִלָּה "word" (מִלַּיָּא רַבְרְבָתָא "the big words" D 7:11), *שְׁנָה "year" (שְׁנִין שַׂגִּיאָן "many years" E 5:11), אֻמָּה, pl. אֻמַּיָּא "nation." There are more such nouns of which forms of the sg. are not found in BA: *כַּוָּה (כַּוִּין פְּתִיחָן "open windows" D 6:11), *אַמָּה (אַמִּין "cubits"), *חִנְטָה (חִנְטִין "wheat").

**62.** Some irregular nouns and adjectives:

*אַב "father" shows long *ū* before pronominal suffixes, except that of the 1. sg.

| | |
|---|---|
| אֲבִי (ʾá*ḇī*) | *אֲבוּנָא |
| אֲבוּךְ | *אֲבוּכֹם (-כוֹן)* |
| *אֲבוּכִי | *אֲבוּכֵן |
| אֲבוּהִי | *אֲבוּהֹם (-הוֹן)* |
| *אֲבוּהַּ | *אֲבוּהֵן |

The pl. is *אֲבָהָן, אֲבָהָתִי, אֲבָהָתָךְ, אֲבָהָתָנָא.

*אַח "brother" does not occur in the sg. with suffixes where its forms would correspond to those of *אַב (*אֲחוּךְ, etc.). The pl. is *אַחִין (ʾa*ḥḥīn*), אֶחָיךְ (ʾe*ḥḥāḵ*) "your colleagues" E 7:18.

*אִנְתָּה "woman, wife" is represented by the pl. *נְשִׁין, נְשֵׁיהוֹן D 6:25, from another root.

*בַּיִת "house" (par. 51) has the pl. *בָּתִּין, בָּתֵּיכוֹן D 2:5. The pronunciation is problematic, probably *bāṯēḵōn*, with exceptional non-spirantization of the *t*.

בַּר "son," with suffix בְּרֵהּ, has the pl. *בְּנִין, בְּנֵי, בְּנוֹהִי, בְּנֵיהוֹן.

יוֹם "day" has the regular pl. יוֹמִין, but יוֹמָת עָלְמָא "days of eternity" E 4:15, 19.

*כְּנֵה (*כְּנָת?) "colleague" has the pl. *כְּנָוָן, כְּנָוָתֵהּ, כְּנָוָתְהוֹן.

מָרֵא "lord," see par. 54.

נְבִזְבָּה "gift" D 2:6 appears in a pl. formation נְבִזְבְּיָתָךְ D 5:17.

עַם, עַמָּא "people" has the pl. עַמְמַיָּא (< *ʿamamayyā*, cf. מַלְכִין < *malaḵīn*, par. 51).

פֶּחָה (*peḥḥā*), cstr. st. פַּחַת (*paḥḥaṯ*), "governor" has the pl. פַּחֲוָתָא.

קִרְיָה (קִרְיָא E 4:15), קִרְיְתָא "city" has a pl. det. st. קִרְיָה: בְּקִרְיָה דִּי שָׁמְרָיִן "in the towns of Samaria" E 4:10.

רֵאשׁ "head" forms the pl. רָאשֵׁיהֹם E 5:10 (as in Hebrew), but also has the normal Aramaic form רֵאשִׁין D 7:6.

רַב, רַבָּא "great, big" forms its pl. with reduplication: רַבְרְבִין, רַבְרְבָן. Used as a noun meaning "chief, magnate," this pl. is further augmented by the ending *-ān*: *רַבְרְבָנִין, רַבְרְבָנַי etc.

רִבּוֹ "myriad" has the pl. רִבְּוָן, i. e., *ribbᵊwān*, but the *qᵊrē* is *riḇᵊḇān*.

שֻׁם "name", with suffix שְׁמֵהּ, has the pl. *שְׁמָהָן, שְׁמָהָת, שְׁמָהָתְהֹם.

שָׁעָה "hour, while," but בַּהּ שַׁעֲתָא "at once" (par. 89).

## VI. Numerals

**63.** Cardinal numbers:

| | masc. | fem. |
|---|---|---|
| 1 | חַד | חֲדָה |
| 2 | *תְּרֵין | תַּרְתֵּין |
| 3 | תְּלָתָה | תְּלָת |
| 4 | אַרְבְּעָה | אַרְבַּע |
| 5 | *חֲמִשָּׁה | *חֲמֵשׁ |
| 6 | *שִׁתָּה | שִׁת (שֵׁת) |
| 7 | שִׁבְעָה | *שְׁבַע |
| 8 | *תְּמָנְיָה | *תְּמָנֵה |
| 9 | *תִּשְׁעָה | *תְּשַׁע |
| 10 | עַשְׂרָה | עֲשַׂר |
| 12 | תְּרֵי עֲשַׂר | |
| 20 | עֶשְׂרִין | |
| 30 | תְּלָתִין | |
| 40 | *אַרְבְּעִין | |
| 50 | *חַמְשִׁין | |

| | |
|---|---|
| 60 | שִׁתִּין |
| 70 | שִׁבְעִין* |
| 80 | תְּמָנִין* |
| 90 | תִּשְׁעִין* |
| 100 | מְאָה |
| 200 | מָאתַ֫יִן |
| 400 | אַרְבַּע מְאָה |
| 1,000 | אֲלַף |
| 10,000 | רִבּוֹ |
| 1,000,000 | אֶ֫לֶף אַלְפִּים (D 7:10, par. 42) |
| 100,000,000 | רִבּוֹ רִבְוָן (par. 62) |

"Sixty-two" (fem.) is שִׁתִּין וְתַרְתֵּין, "120" מְאָה וְעֶשְׂרִין.

**64.** "One" follows the noun as an adjective. It may be used to indicate indetermination (par. 46). It may also be used as a noun: חַד מִנְּהוֹן "one of them" D 6:3. Note also כַּחֲדָה "together, without distinction" D 2:35.

**65.** "Two" has a cstr. st. תְּרֵי, *תַּרְתֵּי.

**66.** The numerals from three to ten use masc. formations (תְּלָת, etc.) with fem. nouns, and fem. formations (תְּלָתָה, etc.) with masc. nouns.

The cstr. st. is rarely used: שִׁבְעַת יָעֲטֹ֫הִי "his seven advisers" E 7:14, but, for instance, שִׁבְעָה עִדָּנִין "seven seasons" D 4:13.

**67.** The numerals may either precede or follow the object counted. The latter is in the plural.

**68.** The det. st. of אֲלַף is אַלְפָּא.

**69.** The ordinal numbers (with the exception of "second") are adjectives with the ending *-āy* (par. 58):

| | masc. | fem. |
|---|---|---|
| 1st | קַדְמָי* (קַדְמָיֵא) | קַדְמָיָה* (קַדְמָיְתָא) |
| 2nd | תִּנְיָן* | תִּנְיָנָה |
| 3rd | תְּלִיתָי* | תְּלִיתָיָה (*tᵊlīṯāʾā*) |
| 4th | רְבִיעָי* (רְבִיעָיָא), etc. | רְבִיעָיָה (רְבִיעָיְתָא), etc. |

**70.** Multiplication is expressed as follows: חַד שִׁבְעָה "seven times" D 3:19.

**71.** Fractions are represented by the nouns פְּלַג "one-half" D 7:25 and תַּלְתָּא "one-third (ruler), triumvir" D 5:16, 29, with suffix תַּלְתִּי D 5:7. The vocalization of תַּלְתָּא may, however, have been influenced by Akkadian *šalšu* and may not represent a genuine Aramaic form.

**72.** "Second" with the adverbial ending *-ūṯ* (par. 88) means "again" (תִּנְיָנוּת D 2:7).

**73.** תְּלָתְהוֹן "the three of them" D 3:23, apparently *tᵊlāṯ-t*, a fem. form, augmented by the ending of the pl. masc., as happens in connection with some prepositions (par. 84).

**74.** Dates: The year of the reign and the day of the month are expressed by cardinal numbers following the cstr. st. שְׁנַת and יוֹם, respectively: שְׁנַת שֵׁת לְמַלְכוּת "year 6 of the reign of . . ." E 6:15, יוֹם תְּלָתָה לִירַח אֲדָר "Adār 3rd" E 6:15.

The age of a person is expressed by the phrase "son of n years": כְּבַר שְׁנִין שִׁתִּין וְתַרְתֵּין "as (a man) sixty-two years old" D 6:1.

## VII. Prepositions

**75.** BA has the primitive prepositions בְּ, כְּ, לְ, מִן, עַד, עַל, עִם, and others whose derivation from nominal or verbal roots is still obvious.

One-consonant prepositions are written together with the word governed by them. This includes מִן wherever *n* is assimilated to the following consonant.

If the first syllable of the word depending on בכל has a murmured vowel, we have -בִּ, -כִּ, -לִ. Followed by יְ, בכל become -בִּי, -כִּי, -לִי.

If the first syllable of the word following בכל has an ultra-short vowel, the corresponding full vowel appears after the preposition: בַּעֲשַׂב "with the vegetation," בֶּאֱסוּר "with a fetter," etc. In connection with אֱלָה "god," it is לֶאֱלָהּ שְׁמַיָּא (יִשְׂרָאֵל) E 5:12, 6:9, 10, 7:15, D 2:19, but usually we find בֵּאלָהֵהּ, לֵאלָהָא, etc.; cf. also בֵּאדַיִן "then."

**76.** Certain basic meanings can be established for the prepositions, but, as is only natural, there are no exact correspondences between a given BA preposition and any one English preposition.

In certain constructions, different prepositions may be used with no clearly definable or necessary distinction in meaning. Instances are the alternation between לְ and עַל to indicate the addressee of a letter or document. Further: לְבַקָּרָה עַל יְהוּד וְלִירוּשְׁלֶם "to investigate Judah and Jerusalem" E 7:14, לְדָנִיֵּאל ... עֲלוֹהִי D 6:5f., עַל עַל (קֳדָם) "to enter into the presence of" in connection with persons, but עַל לְ in connection with localities (D 6:11). Cf. also מְטָה עַד "he came to" D 7:13 in connection with a person, whereas לְ is commonly used with this verb to indicate direction.

שְׁלֵט "to rule over" is usually followed by בְּ, but עַל occurs in D 2:48. *עֲרַב "to mix with" requires בְּ (D 2:41, 43), but עִם is found in D 2:43. עֲדָה "to come forth" is followed by מִן (D 4:28, 5:20) but also by בְּ (D 3:27), if the text is correct. בְּ and מִן also alternate to express the idea of "being wet with the dew (בְּטַל, מִטַּל) of heaven" D 4:12, 20, 22, 30, 5:21.

77. בְּ "in" (local and temporal), "through, with" (instrumental). With suffixes: בִּי, בָּךְ, בֵּהּ, בַּהּ, בְּהוֹן.

Note אִשְׁתִּי בְּ "to drink from (a vessel)" D 5:2, 3, 23, and לָא תִשְׁנֵא צְבוּ בְּדָנִיֵּאל "nothing be changed concerning Daniel" D 6:18.

78. כְּ "like as, comparable to." Also, "according to," as, for instance, repeatedly in כִּדְנָה "thus," כְּדָת מָדַי "according to the law of Media" D 6:9, 13, כִּכְתָב סְפַר מֹשֶׁה "in accordance with the text of the book of Moses" E 6:18. Further, "approximately": כְּשָׁעָה חֲדָה "about an hour (while)" D 4:16.

כְּ may also be used in a temporal sense: כְּבַר שְׁנִין שִׁתִּין וְתַרְתֵּין "as (a man) sixty-two years old" D 6:1, כְּמִקְרְבֵהּ לְגֻבָּא "on approaching the den" D 6:21. Cf. כְּדִי (par. 86).

79. לְ "to, for." With suffixes: לִי, לָךְ, לֵהּ, לַהּ, לַנָא, לְכֹם (לְכוֹן), לְהֹם (לְהוֹן).

לְ expresses every aspect of direction. (a) local: for the addressee of a letter, לְאַרְתַּחְשַׁשְׂתְּא "to Artaxerxes," לְבַיְתֵהּ אֲזַל "he went to his house" D 2:17. (b) temporal: לְעָלְמִין חֱיִי "live for ever." (c) modal: הֲוָת לְטוּר "became a mountain" D 2:35, בֱּנַיְתַהּ לְבֵית מַלְכוּ "I have built it for a royal capital" D 4:27. (d) final: אִמְּרִין לַעֲלָוָן "lambs for sacrifices" E 6:9, מְצַלַּיִן לְחַיֵּי מַלְכָּא "praying for the life of the king" E 6:10.

לְ is commonly used to indicate ownership. It is further used to denote the indirect object and, frequently, the direct object (par. 182). לְ in final meaning usually precedes the infinitive.

**80.** מִן "from." The *n* is sometimes assimilated to the following consonant. With suffixes: מִנִּי, מִנָּךְ, מִנֵּהּ, מִנַּהּ, מִנְּהוֹן, מִנְּהֵן.

מִן indicates local direction away from someone or something. It rarely occurs to express temporal direction (מִן יוֹמָת עָלְמָא "since the days of eternity" E 4:15, 19), or causal relationship (מִן טַעַם אֱלָהּ יִשְׂרָאֵל "by the decree of the God of Israel" E 6:14, 7:23).

In the frequent phrase: מִנִּי שִׂים טְעֵם "an order has been given by me," מִן expresses local direction ("an order . . . coming from me"), cf. the variant מִן קֳדָמַי שִׂים טְעֵם D 6:27, or נִפְקְתָא מִן בֵּית מַלְכָּא תִּתְיְהִב "the expenses will be granted by the royal treasury" E 6:4. However, this usage of מִן comes very close to indicating the agent of the passive.

Partitive use of מִן is common: חַד מִנְּהוֹן "one of them" D 6:3, מִן בְּנֵי גָלוּתָא "belonging to the exiles" D 6:14, מִן נִצְבְּתָא "some of the seed (mineral)" D 2:41, מִן קְשֹׁט "it is of a truth" D 2:47, מִן קְצָת ... מִנַּהּ "partly ... partly" D 2:42. In this sense, מִן also corresponds to "than" after a comparative: בְּחָכְמָה דִּי אִיתַי בִּי מִן כָּל חַיַּיָּא "through wisdom that I have (more) than any living being" D 2:30, חֶזְוַהּ רַב מִן חַבְרָתַהּ "its appearance was great(er) than (that of) its fellows" D 7:20. Cf. also אֲרַע(א) מִנָּךְ "low(er) than you(rs)" D 2:39, עֵלָּא מִנְּהוֹן "high(er) than (above) them" D 6:3.

**81.** עַד "until" (temporal).

It occurs rarely to indicate local direction: עַד עַתִּיק יוֹמַיָּא מְטָה "to the ancient of days he came" D 7:13, עַד כָּה "so far" D 7:28. Modal usage appears in עַד כְּסַף כַּכְּרִין מְאָה "up to one hundred talents of silver" E 7:22. Inclusive finality is intended in עַד יוֹמִין תְּלָתִין "for thirty days" D 6:8, 13.

Note the use of וְ "and" in מִן ... וְעַד "from ... to" E 5:16, D 2:20.

**82.** עַל "upon." With suffixes: עֲלַי, עֲלָךְ, עֲלוֹהִי, עֲלַהּ, עֲלֶינָא, עֲלֵיהֹם (עֲלֵיהוֹן).

In addition to physical location, עַל may indicate mental or modal application: עַל דְּנָה "concerning this" E 4:14, "on account of this" E 4:16, 22, 6:11, עַל רָזָה דְנָה "concerning this secret"

D 2:18, עַל דָּנִיֵּאל שָׂם בָּל "he set his mind on Daniel" D 6:15, בְּאֵשׁ עֲלוֹהִי "it grieved him" D 6:15, טְאֵב עֲלוֹהִי "it pleased him" D 6:24.

עַל may indicate direction like לְ (par. 76): מַנְדְּעִי עֲלַי יְתוּב "my knowledge returned to me" D 4:31, שְׁלַח עַל "to send (a message) to" E 4:11, 5:17. It may involve hostile direction ("against") or indicate superior position and greater intensity: חַד שִׁבְעָה עַל "(heated) seven times more than ..." D 3:19, מִתְנַצַּח עַל סָרְכַיָּא "distinguishing himself over the chief ministers" D 6:4, עַל מַלְכִין מִתְנַשְּׂאָה "(a city) rising up against (raising itself over) kings" E 4:19.

**83.** עִם "together with." With suffixes: עִמִּי, עִמָּךְ, עִמֵּהּ, עִמְּהוֹן.

Temporal use of עִם appears in עִם דָּר וְדָר "in every generation" D 3:33, 4:31, בְּחֶזְוִי עִם לֵילְיָא "in my vision in the night" D 7:2.

Cf., further, עִם מַלְכָּא מַלִּל "he spoke to the king" D 6:22, עָבְדָה קְרָב עִם קַדִּישִׁין "making war against the holy ones" D 7:21, (read שַׁוִּיו?) לִבְבֵהּ עִם חֵיוְתָא שַׁוִּי "his heart (mind) was placed with (= made like) that of an animal" D 5:21, דִּי עֲבַד עִמִּי אֱלָהָא "(wonders that) God did in connection with me" D 3:32, תַּעַבְדוּן עִם שָׂבֵי יְהוּדָיֵא "you shall do in dealing with the elders of the Jews" E 6:8.

**84.** Other prepositions:

אַחֲרֵי "after" (temporal). With suffix: אַחֲרֵיהוֹן.

בָּתַר, בָּאתַר "after" (temporal), < בְּ+אֲתַר, lit. "in the track(s) of." With suffix: בָּתְרָךְ.

בֵּין "between." With suffix: בֵּינֵיהֵן. The forms with pronominal suffixes of בֵּין and some of the following prepositions correspond to those of the *plural* of the masc. noun; they are formed in analogy to עַל.

גּוֹא "within," used in composition with בְּ, לְ, and מִן. With suffixes: בְּגַוַּהּ, בְּגַוַּהּ.

דִּי לָא "without," also used before infinitives introduced by לְ or a prepositional expression.

יַד "hand," in connection with other prepositions, tends to lose its concrete meaning and assume the character of a preposition. בְּיַד indicates possession, cf., in particular, דִּי נִשְׁמְתָךְ בִּידֵהּ וְכָל אֹרְחָתָךְ לֵהּ "(God) who holds in His hand your soul and owns all your ways" D 5:23. Cf. also כְּחָכְמַת אֱלָהָךְ דִּי בִידָךְ "according to the wisdom of your God that is in your hand" E 7:25, יְהַב הִמּוֹ בְּיַד נְבוּכַדְנֶצַּר "He gave them into the hand of Nebuchadnezzar" E 5:12, שֵׁיזִיב ··· מִן יַד אַרְיָוָתָא "he saved . . . from the lions" D 6:28.

יָת indicating the independent objective pronoun occurs only once: יָתְהוֹן D 3:12.

לְוָת "with, at (French *chez*)," related to יָת. With suffix: מִן לְוָתָךְ E 4:12.

נֶגֶד "toward" occurs only in נֶגֶד יְרוּשְׁלֶם "toward Jerusalem" D 6:11, possibly a Hebrew gloss.

צַד "side" in combination with לְ and מִן: מִלִּין לְצַד עִלָּיָא יְמַלִּל "he speaks words toward the Most High" D 7:25, מִצַּד מַלְכוּתָא "(to find cause of complaint against Daniel) from the side of the kingdom (= from the political angle)" D 6:5.

לָקֳבֵל "facing, opposite," also in modal use, "corresponding to." With suffix לָקֳבְלָךְ. In the modal sense, it may be augmented by כְּ: כָּל קֳבֵל.

קֳדָם "before" (local), also with מִן, "from before." With suffixes (par. 10): קֳדָמַי (קֳדָמַי), קֳדָמָךְ (*qŏḏāmāk*), קֳדָמוֹהִי (קֳדָמוֹהִי; וּקְדָמוֹהִי D 7:13), קֳדָמַיהּ, קֳדָמֵיהוֹן. קֳדָם is used frequently as a less direct, respectful indication of location (קֳדָם מַלְכָּא, מִן קֳדָם אֱלָהּ שְׁמַיָּא). A possible temporal use occurs in D 7:7.

מִן קַדְמַת, מִקַּדְמַת "before" (temporal).

לִקְצָת "at the end of."

*תְּחֹת, תְּחוֹת "underneath." With suffixes: תְּחֹתוֹהִי, תַּחְתּוֹהִי.

## VIII. Conjunctions

85. Coordinating conjunctions:

וְ "and," connecting words and sentences, is written together with the word that follows it. If the following word begins with a labial (במפ) or has a murmured vowel in the first syllable, וְ becomes וּ (*ū*). Followed by יְ, *wᵉyᵉ-* becomes וִי-. Followed by a syllable containing an ultra-short vowel, the corresponding full vowel appears after ו: וַהֲלָךְ "and (a kind of) taxes," וֶאֱתוֹ "and come!," etc. However, it is וֵאלָהָא E 6:12 (par. 75), וּסֲגַר "and he locked" D 6:23, וּקְדָמוֹהִי D 7:13.

In Babylonian vocalization, *wᵊ-* remains apparently unchanged before labials and becomes *wi-* before a word with a murmured vowel in the first syllable.

Strings of coordinated nouns or verbs may be without a coordinating particle, or וְ may be used before one, or several, or all components.

בְּרַם, לָהֵן "but." לָהֵן may also be used in the related sense of "except": דִּי לָא יִפְלְחוּן ··· לְכָל אֱלָהּ לָהֵן לֵאלָהֲהוֹן "that they might not worship any God but their own God" D 3:28, מִן כָּל אֱלָהּ וֶאֱנָשׁ ··· לָהֵן מִנָּךְ "from any God or man ... except you" D 6:8, 13.

בֵּאדַיִן, אֱדַיִן "then."

**86.** Subordinating conjunctions:

דִּי "that" introduces subordinate clauses after verbs meaning to know, inform, command, find, see, hear, etc. Cf. also אִיתַי דִּי "it is (a fact) that" E 5:17, מִן קְשֹׁט דִּי "it is of a truth that" D 2:47, אַזְדָּא מִנִּי מִלְּתָא דִּי "the matter is known (as decided), as far as I am concerned, that" D 2:8f. (cf. D 2:5, where the Dead Sea [Qumrān] text inserts די after אזדא).

דִּי is further used to introduce final clauses ("so that" E 5:10, 6:10, D 2:18, 3:28, 6:18). It is causal in D 2:47, 4:15, 6:24. It may also introduce direct speech (D 2:25, 5:7, 6:6, 8, 14). Note בְּעִדָּנָא דִּי "at the time when" D 3:5, 15.

כְּדִי "when" (temporal, but tending occasionally toward a causal meaning).

מִן דִּי "after, as soon as," occasionally causal as in D 3:22.

כָּל קֳבֵל דִּי "because," but in D 5:22 "although."

הֵא כְדִי "as" D 2:43, spelled as if it were **hā-kᵊdī*, but to be pronounced as derived from *hēk-dī*.

עַד דִּי "until," also simple עַד E 4:21, 5:5, tending toward a final connotation in D 4:22.

עַל דִּבְרַת דִּי (D 2:30), עַד דִּבְרַת דִּי (D 4:14) (= *ʿaddibrat* < *ʿal-dibrat*) "so that."

לְמָה (E 4:22), דִּי לְמָה (E 7:23) "lest."

הֵן "if." In D 3:15 (הֵן ··· הֵן לָא "if . . . if not"), the apodosis for the positive alternative is left unstated (supply "it is well and good"). הֵן ··· הֵן may mean "either . . . or": הֵן לְמוֹת הֵן לִשְׁרֹשִׁי הֵן לַעֲנָשׁ נִכְסִין וְלֶאֱסוּרִין "(will be sentenced) either to death or to corporal punishment or to a property fine and imprisonment" E 7:26.

## IX. Negations

87. לָא is used in connection with negative statements. It may also be used for the negation of individual parts of a sentence.

It is used as a noun in כָּל דָּאְרֵי אַרְעָא כְּלָה חֲשִׁיבִין (*dāy*ᵊ*rē*) "all inhabitants of the earth are considered like nought" D 4:32.

אַל is used with the jussive to express a negative wish or command. The imperative cannot be employed with negation. אַל was discarded in later Aramaic and replaced by לָא. A possible but doubtful example of this process in E 4:21: קִרְיְתָא דָךְ לָא תִתְבְּנֵא "let that city not be rebuilt."

For לְמָה "lest," cf. par. 86, and for דִּי לָא "without" (also simple לָא before an infinitive, D 6:16), cf. par. 84.

## X. Adverbs and Particles

88. Adverbs may be expressed by prepositional expressions or by special words. In addition, they may be formed by

(1) an ancient fem. formation showing retention of final *-t*: טְוָת "(he spent the night) fasting" D 6:19.

(2) the ending *-ūṯ*: תִּנְיָנוּת "a second time, again" D 2:7.

(3) the abs. st. masc., as in the frequent שַׂגִּיא "much, greatly, very": קְצַף שַׂגִּיא "he became very angry" D 2:12, שַׂגִּיא מִתְבַּהַל "greatly disturbed" D 5:9 (par. 20), etc. A further example may be גְּמִיר "completely" (= and so on, with all the proper formulas of greeting to be supplied) E 7:12.

(4) the ending *-ā*, mostly unstressed, the remnant of an ancient accusative ending: אֵזֵא יַתִּירָא "heated excessively" D 3:22, תַּקִּיפָא (*yattīrā́*!) יַתִּירָא "exceedingly strong" (fem.) D 7:7, דְּחִילָה יַתִּירָה "very frightening" (fem.) D 7:19. Further, אַרְעָא (*ʾárʿā*, read *ʾaraʿ*) "below" and עֵלָּא "above" (par. 80), and, possibly, יַצִּיבָא in D 3:24, יַצִּיבָא מַלְכָּא (*yaṣṣībā́*!) "certainly, O king" (cf. מִן יַצִּיב יָדַע אֲנָה "I know for certain" D 2:8). For כְּלָא, see par. 96. The final *-ā* of some Persian loan words was apparently considered the same ending (par. 189).

**89.** Temporal demonstrative adverbs:

אֱדַ֫יִן, בֵּאדַ֫יִן "then," used by itself as a coordinating conjunction (par. 85), but וְאֱדַ֫יִן "and then" E 5:5.

כְּעַן, כְּעֶ֫נֶת (E 4:10, 11, 7:12), כְּעֶת (E 4:17) "now, now then."

עַד אָחֳרֵין "eventually" D 4:5.

בַּהּ זִמְנָא, בַּהּ שַׁעֲתָא "at once," lit. "at this very hour (time, moment)." ה here represents the demonstrative element *hā* and was assimilated to the pronominal suffixes (par. 32), used in the proleptic manner found, for instance, in בֵּהּ בְּלֵילְיָא "in this very night" D 5:30 and בֵּהּ בְּדָנִיֵּאל "in Daniel" D 5:12. The demonstrative construction is still reflected in מִנַּהּ מַלְכוּתָה "from (this) kingdom" D 7:24.

**90.** Temporal assertive adverb:

עוֹד "still, yet": עוֹד מִלְּתָא בְּפֻם מַלְכָּא "the word still (being) in the mouth of the king" D 4:28.

**91.** Local demonstrative adverbs:

הָא "behold here": הָא אֲנָה חָזֵה "behold, I see" D 3:25.

אֲלוּ, אֲרוּ "behold there (is)," always preceded by *wa-*.

כָּה "here" D 7:28.

תַּמָּה "there," מִן תַּמָּה "from there."

אֲתַר דִּי "there where," lit., "on the spot where" E 6:3, a use possibly influenced by Akkadian *ašar* "where."

**92.** Modal demonstrative adverbs:

כִּדְנָה, כֵּן, כְּנֵ֫מָא "thus."

כְּמָה "how!": אָתוֹהִי כְּמָה רַבְרְבִין וְתִמְהוֹהִי כְּמָה תַקִּיפִין "how great are His wonders, and how mighty are His miracles!" D 3:33.

**93.** Modal assertive adverbs:

אַף "also."

אָפְּתֹם "certainly" or "finally" E 4:13 (par. 190).

אָסְפַּ֫רְנָא (*ʾospárnā*) "exactly, perfectly" (par. 189).

אַדְרַזְדָּא "diligently" (par. 189).

10 הַצְדָּא D 3:14 is often explained as the interrogative particle with an adverb *צדא, possibly meaning "truly" (?).

כַּחֲדָה "together, without distinction" (par. 64).

אֱזְדָּא "publicly known, known (as decided)" (par. 189) is originally an adverb.

**94.** The interrogative particle is -הֲ, with the negation הֲלָא. -הַ for -הֲ is found before words with a murmured vowel in the first syllable and before words beginning with א. Presumably, -הַ would also appear before words beginning with a laryngal.

## XI. אִיתַי

**95.** אִיתַי indicates existence ("there is, exists"), or, with negation, non-existence (לָא אִיתַי "there does not exist"). In this meaning, אִיתַי remains unchanged. Cf. אִיתַי גֻּבְרִין יְהוּדָאיִן "there are Jewish men" D 3:12, חָכְמָה דִּי אִיתַי בִּי "wisdom that exists in me" D 2:30; further, הֵן אִיתַי דִּי "whether it is (a fact) that" E 5:17.

However, אִיתַי may take the place of the copula (which, as a rule, is left unexpressed in BA, or is expressed by the independent personal pronoun [par. 30]). In this case, it takes the appropriate pronominal suffix. Originally, אִיתַי here was used for emphasis: הַאִיתָךְ כָּהֵל "*are* you able?" D 2:26, מְדָרְהוֹן עִם בִּשְׂרָא לָא אִיתוֹהִי "their dwelling is *not* with human kind" D 2:11, לָא אִיתַנָא פָלְחִין "we shall *not* worship" D 3:18, לָא אִיתֵיכוֹן פָּלְחִין "you do *not* worship" D 3:14, אִיתֵיכוֹן עֲתִידִין "you *are* ready" D 3:15.

## XII. כֹּל and אָחֳרָן

**96.** כֹּל (unstressed כָּל) is a noun meaning "totality." Cf. כֹּלָּא (*kọllā*) "everything, everyone" D 2:40, 4:9, 18, 25. This form may also be used in a quasi-adverbial manner: שְׁלָמָא כֹלָּא "well-being completely" E 5:7.

Preceding a sg. noun without the article, it means "every, any." Preceding a determined noun in the sg., it means "entire, whole." And preceding a determined noun in the pl. or a collective sg. (i.e., כָּל בִּשְׂרָא "all mankind"), or being followed by the pl. of the pronominal suffix, or the relative pronoun, or the demonstrative pronoun used as a noun (כָּל דְּנָה "all this"), it means "all."

Note that כָּל קֳבֵל has nothing to do with כֹּל (par. 84).

**97.** אָחֳרָן "other" may be used either as a noun or as an adjective. Its fem. is אָחֳרִי (par. 57).

## XIII. The Verb

**98.** The BA verb possesses two tenses: a "perfect" to indicate completed action, corresponding to the English present perfect, simple past, and past perfect, and an "imperfect" to indicate incomplete ("im-perfect") action, corresponding to our present or future. It further has a participle, which moreover serves widely as a multi-purpose tense (par. 177). It has two moods, an imperative and a jussive; and an infinitive. There are two voices, active and passive.

**99.** In addition to its basic form, the BA verb has two "derived conjugations," that is, modifications of the basic root to express modes of action. This is achieved by doubling of the second consonant of the root, or by the addition of a prefix. Each conjugation, furthermore, can form a reflexive/passive by prefixing the element *t-* (*hiṯ-*, *ʾiṯ-*). Thus, the conjugations are:

| | | | | |
|---|---|---|---|---|
| | pᵊʿal | hiṯpᵊʿẹl | Passive: | pᵊʿīl |
| 11 | paʿʿẹl | hiṯpaʿʿal | | *puʿʿal |
| | hap̄ʿẹl | *hiṯhap̄ʿal | | hu/op̄ʿal |

The basic meaning of the paʿʿẹl is intensive or causative, and that of the hap̄ʿẹl, causative.

12 Beginning *h* alternates with the glottal stop, but forms with *h* are more widely used in the BA text.

Since the reflexive of the hap̄ʿẹl is not attested in BA (except by doubtful textual correction of E 4:13, מַלְכִים תְּהַנְזִק to מַלְכֵי מתהנזק), its form is somewhat uncertain.

For remnants of the šap̄ʿẹl (corresponding in meaning to the hap̄ʿẹl) and hištap̄ʿal, cf. par. 157 and 166.

**100.** The verbal conjugation follows an identical scheme for all roots. Minor irregularities occur principally in connection with roots that contain a glottal stop; that have *n* as the first consonant; and which consisted originally of two consonants made triconsonantal by the addition of *w/y* or by doubling of the second consonant. These are the "weak" verbs, as opposed to the regular "strong" verb.

### 1. The strong verb

Cf. the paradigms, pp. 64—67.

**101.** The perfect is formed with the help of suffixed elements:

| | | | |
|---|---|---|---|
| sg. | 3. masc. | | כְּתַב |
| | 3. fem. | *-aṯ* | כִּתְבַת |
| | 2. masc. | *-t* (*-tā*) | כְּתַבְתְּ (כְּתַבְתָּ, -תָּה) |
| | 2. fem. | *-tī* | כְּתַבְתִּי* |
| | 1. | *-ẹṯ* | כִּתְבֵת |
| pl. | 3. masc. | *-ū* | כְּתַבוּ |
| | 3. fem. | *-ā* (par. 12) | כְּתַבָה |
| | 2. masc. | *-tūn* | כְּתַבְתּוּן |
| | 2. fem. | *-tẹn* | כְּתַבְתֵּן |
| | 1. | *-nā* | כְּתַבְנָא |

**102.** In addition to the p$^{\text{əʿ}}$al with *a* in the second syllable, there also exists a p$^{\text{əʿ}}$ẹ/il: סְגִד "prostrated himself," שְׁלִם "was completed," שְׁלֵט "had power," pl. שְׁלִטוּ. For the 3. fem. sg., besides תִּקְפַת (from תְּקֵף "was strong"), we find בְּטֵלַת "was idle." The vocalization בְּטֵלַת corresponds to what in later Jewish Aramaic is the normal vocalization of the 3. fem. sg. (*p$^{\text{əʿ}}$a/ẹlaṯ*).

For the passive forms and the derived conjugations, cf. the paradigms.

**103.** *ẹ* and *i* may apparently be used interchangeably in the p$^{\text{əʿ}}$ẹl, hiṯp$^{\text{əʿ}}$ẹl, paʿʿẹl, and hap̄ʿẹl.

**104.** The 3. fem. sg. of the derived conjugations is attested only with verbs ending in laryngals or *r* and other weak verbs

(הִתְגְּזֶרֶת, הַדֶּקֶת, etc.). These forms do not seem normative (at least, not for the period of Official Aramaic), and the normal form presumably was *הִתְכַּתְבַת, etc.

**105.** The imperfect (jussive, par. 108) uses prefixes, supplemented in some of its forms by suffixes:

| | | | |
|---|---|---|---|
| sg. | 3. masc. | *y-* | יִכְתֻּב |
| | 3. fem. | *t-* | תִּכְתֻּב |
| | 2. masc. | *t-* | תִּכְתֻּב |
| | 2. fem. | *t---īn* | *תִּכְתְּבִין |
| | 1. | *ʾ-* | אֶכְתֻּב |
| pl. | 3. masc. | *y---ūn* | יִכְתְּבוּן |
| | 3. fem. | *y---ān* | יִכְתְּבָן |
| | 2. masc. | *t---ūn* | תִּכְתְּבוּן |
| | 2. fem. | *t---ān* | *תִּכְתְּבָן |
| | 1. | *n-* | נִכְתֻּב |

For the use of the prefix *l-*, instead of *y-*, see par. 168.

**106.** No practical rules can be formulated for the vowel following the second consonant of the root. Most verbs pᵊʿal have *u*. Pᵊʿẹl verbs prefer *a*, but cf., for instance, סְגִד — יִסְגֻּד. For imperfects with *ẹ*, cf. par. 118.

**107.** No passive forms of the imperfect happen to occur in BA.

**108.** The jussive is indicated only in a few forms by the elision of final *-n* in the 3. masc. pl. Only weak verbs happen to be attested: יֵאבַדוּ "let them perish" Jer. 10:11, אַל יִשְׁתַּנּוֹ "let them not be changed" D 5:10, with pronominal suffix אַל יְבַהֲלוּךְ "let them not disturb you" D 5:10. The form of the suffix in אַל יְבַהֲלָךְ "let it not disturb you" D 4:16 indicates the jussive, as the indicative would be *יְבַהֲלִנָּךְ (par. 175). Finally, the spelling with final *-y* in יִתְקְרֵי "let him be called" D 5:12 may be the remnant of an old jussive form (par. 152).

**109.** In the hiṯpᵊʿẹl and hiṯpaʿʿal, the imperfect prefix + *(h)iṯ-* becomes *yiṯ-*, etc. In the hapʿẹl, *h* is retained, but the ʾapʿẹl has the imperfect *ya-*, etc.

**110.** The imperative has the same vowel after the second consonant of the root as is found in the imperfect (jussive), and endings corresponding to those of the jussive:

| | | |
|---|---|---|
| sg. 2. masc. | | כְּתֻב, שְׁלַט |
| 2. fem. | -ī | כְּתֻבִי |
| pl. 2. masc. | -ū | כְּתֻבוּ |
| 2. fem. | -ā | כְּתֻבָה* |

The imperative cannot be used in connection with a negation. In order to express a negated imperative, the jussive (imperfect) must be used (par. 87).

**111.** The infinitive of the pᵊʿal has the preformative *m*- (מִכְתַּב). A remnant of an older form without *m*- is לְבְּנֵא (par. 149).

In the derived conjugations, a fem. formation serves as infinitive (*p...ʿālā*). The cstr. st. ending *-aṯ* is preserved only in לְהַנְזָקַת מַלְכִין "to cause harm to kings" E 4:22 and אַחֲוָיַת אֲחִידָן "giving information on riddles" D 5:12. Elsewhere, it is replaced by *-ūṯ*, for instance, הִתְנַדָּבוּת "contributing" E 7:16, לְהוֹדָעוּתָךְ "to let you know" E 5:10.

Forms such as מַצְלְחָה "to succeed" E 5:8 and מְפַשַּׁר "to interpret," מְשְׁרֵא "to solve" D 5:12, may be further infinitive formations of the derived conjugations, but this is uncertain, as is the assumption that אֶשְׁתַּדּוּר "rebellion" E 4:15 is an infinitive of the hiṯpaʿʿal of the root שׁדר (cf. par. 190 for a Persian etymology).

**112.** The participles may be used and declined as any noun or adjective.

**113.** For the addition of pronominal suffixes, cf. par. 174ff. and the paradigms, p. 75.

2. Roots beginning with a sibilant or dental

**114.** The reflexive *t* is placed after the sibilant: מִשְׁתַּבְּשִׁין "confused," תִּשְׁתְּבִק "will be left," הִשְׁתְּכַח "was found," מִשְׂתַּכַּל "observing."

It assimilates to the emphatic pronunciation of צ and becomes ט: יִצְטַבַּע "will be wetted."

It assimilates fully to ז in הִזְדְּמִנְתּוּן "you have agreed upon" D 2:9. The written form represents *hizzᵉmintūn* or *hizzammintūn*, while the reading prescribed assumes only partial assimilation of *t* > *d*, *hizdᵊmintūn*.

The situation is different with roots having *w*/*y* as the second consonant (par. 138).

Assimilation can also be expected in roots beginning with a dental, but no relevant forms are found in BA.

### 3. Roots containing a laryngal or ר

**115.** In connection with these roots, note the rules mentioned in par. 24 (preceding *ẹ*/*i* > *a*) and par. 20 (lengthening of preceding vowel instead of gemination): פָּלַח "worshiping," מְשַׁבַּח "praising" (identical in form with the passive participle), אָמַר "saying," בָּרֵךְ (< *barrik*) "he blessed," etc.

In roots ending in a laryngal or ר, the change *ẹ*/*i* > *a* is extended to open syllables: שַׁבַּחוּ "they praised," הַשְׁכַּחוּ "they found," אַתַּרוּ "shake off!" (pl.), בַּדַּרוּ "scatter!" (pl.), אֶתְעֲקַרָה "they (fem.) were uprooted."

**116.** In addition, the following differences affecting the vocalization may be noted:

Roots with a laryngal as the first consonant have *a* in the perfect pᵊʿal, 1. sg. (and 3. fem. sg.): עַבְדֵת "I have made."

The prefix vowel of the imperfect is *a* (*e* in verbs with ʾ/*w*/*y* as the third consonant of the root): תַּעַבְדוּן "you will do," תֶּעְדֵּא "it (fem.) will pass away."

The prefix vowel of the infinitive is *e*: לְמֶעְבַּד "to do," לְמֶחֱזֵא "to behold."

Where the laryngal is originally vowelless after a prefix and the following consonant has a murmured vowel, the laryngal may take the vowel of the prefix: תַּעַבְדוּן (< *taʿbᵉdūn*), הָחָרְבַת (*hoḥorḇaṯ* < *hoḥrᵊḇaṯ*) "was destroyed". But cf. יַחְסְנוּן "they will possess," מְהַחְצְפָה "urgent" (fem.).

*e* for *a* occurs in הֶחֱסִנוּ "they took possession" D 7:22, הֶעְדִּיו "they removed" D 5:20, 7:12.

**117.** Roots ending in a laryngal or ר tend to eliminate a final cluster of consonants, such as is usual in the 2. masc. sg. of the perfect, by the insertion of an anaptyctic vowel: הִשְׁתְּכַ֫חַתְּ "you were found" D 5:27 (but, with retention of the final vowel, שַׁבַּ֫חְתָּ "you praised" D 5:23). Cf. the similar phenomenon in the noun (par. 51).

This vocalization has been transferred to the 3. fem. sg. and 1. sg.: אֲמֶ֫רֶת "she said" D 5:10, (-אִת) הִתְגְּזֶ֫רֶת "it (fem.) broke off" D 2:34, 45, הִשְׁתְּכַ֫חַת "it (fem.) was found" D 5:11, etc., הַשְׁכַּ֫חַת "I have found" D 2:25. However, we also find יִדְעֵת "I knew," שַׁבְּחֵת "I praised." Cf. also שָׂ֫מֶת, הֲקֵ֫מֶת, הַדֶּ֫קֶת (par. 133, 140, 164).

### 4. Roots beginning with נ

**118.** In connection with these roots, cf. par. 21 (assimilation/nasalization of vowelless *n*): יִנְתְּנוּן "they will give" E 4:13, but also יִתְּנִנַּהּ "he gives it" D 4:14, 22, 29.

*ẹ* as the vowel of the imperfect p^əʿal is found in נפל "to fall" and נתן "to give": יִפֵּל (unstressed יִפֶּל לָךְ *yippellā́ḵ* E 7:20), יִנְתֵּן, תִּנְתֵּן. Cf. also שֵׂא "take!" (par. 126).

Only the imperfect and the infinitive of the root נתן occur in BA; for the perfect and imperative, another root, יהב, is used (par. 129).

**119.** The imperative drops the נ: פֻּ֫קוּ "come out!" (pl.) D 3:26, שֵׂא "take!" E 5:15.

### 5. Roots beginning with א

**120.** The vowel *a* appears in the p^əʿal perfect, 1. sg.: אַמְרֵת "I said" D 4:5. For the 3. fem. sg., where the same vocalization can be expected (*אַמְרַת), the only example available is again from a root ending in ר: אֲמֶ֫רֶת "she said" D 5:10 (par. 117).

**121.** In the imperfect and infinitive of the p^əʿal, the vowelless glottal stop becomes silent, and the preceding vowel is lengthened: יֵאמַר, נֵאמַר, תֵּאמְרוּן, יֵאבַ֫דוּ "let them perish" Jer. 10:11, מֵאמַר (מֵמַר E 5:11), לְמֵזֵא "to heat" D 3:19.

**122.** The imperative p^əʿal with *a* after the second consonant has ^e in the first syllable, the one with *u* has ^a: אֱמַר, אֱמַ֫רוּ, but אֲכֻ֫לִי "eat!" (fem.) D 7:5.

Full *ẹ* (with secondary stress) appears in the case of an imperative with *e* after the second consonant: אֵזֶל (ʾẹ̀zel-) "go!" E 5:15.

**123.** The part. pass. pᵊʿal can be expected to have been *אֲמִיר, but *ẹ* appears in the first syllable of the only form attested (of a root ending in *w*/*y*): אֵזֵה "heated" D 3:22.

**124.** In the hap̄ʿẹl, *hǭ-* (< *haw-*) replaces **haʾ*: *הוֹבֵד, תְּהוֹבֵד, יְהוֹבְדוּן, לְהוֹבָדָה "to destroy." The passive is הוּבַד "was destroyed" D 7:11.

Two roots, אמן and אתה, show *hē-* and *hay-*: הֵימִן "he believed" D 6:24, מְהֵימַן "trusted, trustworthy" D 2:45, 6:5, הַיְתִי "he brought," passive הֵיתָיִת, הֵיתָיו (par. 167).

6. Roots with א as the second consonant

**125.** None of the forms attested shows any irregularity: שְׁאֵל "he asked," שְׁאֵלְנָא, שָׁאֵל, יִשְׁאֲלֶנְכוֹן "he will ask you," בְּאֵשׁ "was bad," טְאֵב "was good."

7. Roots with final א

**126.** Most of these roots have merged with those originally ending in *w*/*y*. Since their forms can no longer be distinguished from those of the latter, they are treated together with them (par. 144ff.).

Remnants of roots ending in א that have preserved א as a consonant are נשׂא (שֵׂא "take!" E 5:15, מִתְנַשְּׂאָה "rising up" [fem.] E 4:19) and שׂנא "to hate" (שָׂנְאָךְ "your enemies" D 4:16).

8. Roots beginning with י

**127.** In Aramaic (and Canaanite), initial *w* has been replaced by *y*, so that all roots originally beginning with *w* have merged with those beginning with *y*.

**128.** In the imperfect (and infinitive) of the pᵊʿal, vowelless י is replaced by gemination/nasalization of the second consonant in the ancient roots יְדַע "to know" and יְתִב "to sit": יִנְדְּעוּן, תִּנְדַּע, אִנְדַּע, יִתִּב D 7:26; cf. also the noun מַנְדַּע "knowledge." Further יִכֻּל, from the root יְכִל "to be able" (par. 171).

Another imperfect formation is attested only through יֵיטַב "it is good, pleases" E 7:18, from an ancient secondary root יטב (cf. טְאֵב, טָב).

**129.** Verbs forming the imperfect with gemination/nasalization of the second consonant drop י in the imperative: דַּע "know!" D 6:16, הַב "give!" D 5:17 (from the root יהב which, for the imperfect and infinitive, is replaced by נתן [par. 118]). Cf. also the nouns עֵטָה "advice," שְׁנָתֵהּ "his sleep," representing old infinitive formations of יעט, ישן.

**130.** The hap̄ʿel has *hō-* (< *haw-*): הוֹדַע "he informed," יְהוֹדַע, מְהוֹדְעִין, לְהוֹדָעָה, הוֹתֵב "he settled (them)," מְהוֹדֵא, מוֹדֵא "praising." The passive is הוּסְפַת "was added" (fem.) D 4:33.

*hē-* is found only in הֵיבֵל "he brought" E 5:14, לְהֵיבָלָה E 7:15. The same root may be present also in מְסוֹבְלִין "(foundations) laid" *11*
E 6:3, as a šap̄ʿel borrowed from Akkadian (par. 188).

9. Roots with ו or י as the second consonant

Cf. the paradigms, pp. 68—69.

**131.** Formations of roots with *y* as the second consonant have, in many instances, become identical with those of roots containing *w*. Therefore, it is convenient to treat the two groups of verbs together.

**132.** In some roots, ו functions as a consonant: תְּוַהּ "he was perturbed" and, in roots with final *y*, הֲוָה "he was," *חַוִּי "he informed," שַׁוִּי, יְשְׁתַּוֵּה "to place, make."

**133.** Long *ā* is found throughout the perfect pᵊʿal: קָם "he rose" (root *qwm*), שָׂם "he placed" (root *śym*), בָּת "he spent the night" (root *byt*). A pᵊʿe/il is רֵם "(his heart) was haughty" (root *rwm*) D 5:20.

The 1. sg. is שָׂמֶת (< *śāmt*) E 6:12.

There is a passive form שָׂמַת "it (fem.) was placed" D 6:18. This makes it doubtful whether the frequent שִׂים is a perfect passive, or rather the participle passive.

**134.** The imperfect pᵊʿal has *ū* throughout (יְקוּם), and, presumably, *ī* in roots containing *y* (*יְשִׂים). An *ā* imperfect occurs in יְהָךְ "he will go" (par. 169).

**135.** The imperative is *קוּם, קוּמִי, and *שִׂים, שִׂימוּ.

**136.** The infinitive has the form *מְקָם, *מְשָׂם, cf. מְהָךְ (par. 169).

**137.** In the active participle of the p<sup>ə</sup>ʿal, *w*/*y* is replaced by the glottal stop (קָאֵם). In the other forms where א has a murmured vowel, א remains in writing, but the reading prescribed by the Masoretes is י: קָאְמִין (*qāyᵊmīn*), דָּאְנִין (*dāyᵊnīn*) "judging," דָּאְרֵי (*dāyᵊrē*) "dwellers of." But קָאֲמַיָּא D 7:16, where the main word stress does not immediately follow the syllable containing ʾ/*y*.

**138.** The hiṯpᵊʿel shows gemination of the preformative *t*, and either *ī* or *ā* after the first consonant of the root: יִתְּזִין "obtains food" D 4:9, but יִתְּשָׂם, מִתְּשָׂם.

**139.** The paʿʿel of *qwm* is *קַיֵּם, לְקַיָּמָה, with י instead of ו. In all other respects, both paʿʿel and hiṯpaʿʿal of these roots are like those of the strong verb.

**140.** The perfect of the hap̄ʿel shows vacillation between *ī* and *ē* after the first consonant of the root: הֲקֵים, אֲקִימֵהּ "he set (it) up." The 1. sg. is הֲקֵימֶת D 3:14.

The passive is הֳקָמַת (fem.) D 7:5, הֳקִימַת D 7:4. It has been suggested that the first form be read *הֳקָמַת (and be transferred to D 7:4), and the second as the active *הֲקִימַת (and be transferred to D 7:5).

**141.** The imperfect, the participle, and, presumably, the imperative of the hap̄ʿel show the same vacillation between *ī* and *ē*. In addition, an unusual long *ā* (par. 23) appears after the preformative in some cases: יְתִיבוּן, יַהֲתִיבוּן "they will return, give back" E 5:5, 6:5, יְקִים, יְהָקֵים, מְהָקֵים, תָּסֵיף "it (fem.) will bring to an end," מְרִים "raising up," מְגִיחָן "stirring up" (pl. fem.).

**142.** The infinitive of the hap̄ʿel is לַהֲזָדָה "to act impiously" D 5:20, לַהֲקָמוּתֵהּ "to set him up" D 6:4, לַהֲתָבוּתָךְ "to render (a reply) to you" D 3:16.

**143.** A remnant of a derived conjugation, formed with reduplication of the last consonant, appears in מְרוֹמֵם "exalting" D 4:34, הִתְרוֹמַמְתָּ "you exalted yourself" D 5:23 (cf. par. 157).

## 10. Roots ending in ו/י or א

Cf. the paradigms, pp. 70—72.

**144.** Roots originally ending in ו/י and א have merged in BA, with some isolated exceptions for those ending in א (par. 126).

The spelling of final *ā* and *ẹ̄* in forms of these roots vacillates between ה and א.

**145.** The pəʿal has two formations in the perfect, corresponding to pəʿal and pəʿẹ/il. The second is represented only by the forms אִשְׁתִּיו "they drank" D 5:3 f. and צְבִית "I wished" D 7:19.

The perfect of the pəʿal formation has the endings *-ā*, *-āṯ*, and *-ọ̄* for the 3. masc. sg., 3. fem. sg., and 3. masc. pl., respectively. The diphthong *ay* is retained in the 2. sg., but contracted to *ẹ̄* in the 2. pl. and the 1. sg. and pl.

Note רְבַית "you have grown" D 4:19, where the consonants indicate the usual form רְבַ֫יְתָ, while the reading suggested is רְבַת. הֲוָת "it (fem.) was" D 2:35 is doubtful and, probably, should be הֲוָת. 13

**146.** The passive pəʿal is represented by גְּלִי, גֱּלִי, "was revealed," and קֱרִי "was read."

**147.** The imperfect forms without suffixed elements end in *-ẹ̄* (< *-ay*). The 2. and 3. masc. pl. end in *-ọ̄n* (< *-awn* < *-ayūn*), while the corresponding fem. forms retain *y* as a consonant. However, the 2. masc. pl. with pronominal suffix is תְּהַחֲוֻנַּ֫נִי (*təhaḥawunnánī* [par. 175]) "you will let me know" D 2:9, with *u* instead of *ọ̄*/*ọ*.

For forms with the prefix *l-* in connection with הוה, see par. 168.

**148.** The imperative pəʿal is represented by חֱיִי "live!," הֱווֹ "be!" (pl.) E 4:22 (הֱוֹו E 6:6), אֱתוֹ "come!" (pl.) D 3:26.

**149.** The infinitive pəʿal ends in *-ẹ̄* (< *-ay*): לְמִבְנֵא "to build." An ancient form without preformative is attested in לִבְנֵא E 5:3,13 (originally *bənā?*). A form expanded into the det. st. is לְמִבְנְיָה E 5:9.

Forms with pronominal suffixes restore *y*: כְּמִצְבְּיֵהּ "as he wishes" D 4:32, לְמֵזְיֵהּ "to heat it" D 3:19.

**150.** The active participle is (עָנֵא) עָנֵה "answering," fem. שָׁנְיָה "being different," pl. masc. שָׁתַ֫יִן "drinking," fem. שָׁנְיָן "being different."

The passive participle is שְׁרֵא "residing," בְּנֵה "built" (בְּנַ֫יִן, בְּנַיָה, בְּנַיָן).

**151.** The perfect of the derived conjugations ends in *-ī*, retained throughout.

The 3. fem. sg. is represented only by the (h)iṯpəʿel אֶתְכְּרִיַּת "(my spirit) became sick" D 7:15. Whether this vocalization is exceptional, instead of an expected *הִתְבְּנִית, or whether it is to be considered the normal form in BA (as it is in later Jewish Aramaic) cannot now be decided (par. 102, 104, 117).

The passive of a derived conjugation is represented by הֵיתָ֫יִת הֵיתָ֫יו (par. 167).

**152.** The formation of the imperfect of the derived conjugations corresponds to that of the pᵊʿal.

A jussive is attested in אַל יִשְׁתַּנּוֹ "let them not be changed" D 5:10. In יִתְקְרֵי "let him be called" D 5:12, the spelling with י, instead of א/ה, may indicate a jussive, although such orthographic distinction had become obscured already at an early date.

**153.** The imperative of the derived conjugations is attested by מֶ֫נִּי (*ménnī*) "appoint!" E 7:25 and הַחֲוֹ֫נִי "let me know!" (pl.) D 2:6.

**154.** The infinitives of the derived conjugations retain י as a consonant.

**155.** The endings of the active participles of the derived conjugations correspond to those of the pᵊʿal. The sg. masc. of the passive participles of the paʿʿẹl and the hap̄ʿẹl may have been **מְבַנַּי, **מְהַבְנַי.

**156.** For the addition of pronominal suffixes, see par. 176 and the paradigms, p. 75.

### 11. Roots with identical second and third consonants

Cf. the paradigms, pp. 73—74.

**157.** Certain verbs of this type seem to have been treated like the strong verb, cf. the (h)ap̄ʿẹl תַּטְלֵל ("the animals) seek shade (shelter)" D 4:9. This applies to the šap̄ʿẹl, borrowed from Akkadian,
14 שַׁכְלִ֫לוּ "they completed," שַׁכְלְלֵהּ "he completed it," לְשַׁכְלָלָה, יִשְׁתַּכְלְלוּן. It also applies to formations such as אֶשְׁתּוֹמַם "he was perturbed" (root *šmm*) D 4:16 and מְרוֹמֵם, הִתְרוֹמַּמְתָּ (par. 143).

**158.** The perfect pᵊʿal shows contraction of the identical consonants in the 3. masc. sg. and pl. Contraction also takes place in other forms where the two identical consonants are separated only by a murmured vowel reduced to zero, but original separatedness may be indicated in the written form: עַל "he entered," עַלַלַת (*ʿalᵊlat̲*, read *ʿallat̲*) "she entered" D 5:10, but נַדַּת "(his sleep) fled" D 6:19. דָּקוּ "they were crushed" D 2:35 (as if derived from a root *dwq*) should be דַּקּוּ.

**159.** The imperfect, and all other forms with preformatives, are characterized by transference of the gemination from the second/third to the first consonant of the root: תֵּרֹעַ (< *tirroᵃʿ*) "(the kingdom) will break" D 2:40. Cf. also the noun מֶעָלֵי (*mèʿʿālē̩*) "the entrance (setting) of (the sun)" D 6:15.

**160.** The imperative shows contraction as in the perfect: גֹּדּוּ "cut down!" (pl.) D 4:11, 20.

**161.** The infinitive is attested in מִחַן (*miḥḥan*) "to show mercy" D 4:24.

**162.** The active participle pᵊʿal is formed like that of the strong verb, but the *kᵊt̲īb̲* suggests contraction for forms augmented by endings: עָלְלִין (*ʿālᵊlīn*, read *ʿāllīn*) "entering" (pl.) D 4:4, 5:8.

**163.** The hit̲pᵊʿe̩l is not attested. All forms of the paʿʿe̩l and the hit̲paʿʿal correspond to those of the strong verb.

**164.** The hap̄ʿe̩l requires gemination/nasalization of the first consonant of the root (par. 159): הַנְעֵל "he brought in" D 2:25, הַעֵלְנִי "let me enter!" D 2:24, הַדֵּקֶת, הַדֶּקֶת "it (fem.) crushed" D 2:34, 45, הַדִּקוּ D 6:25, תַּדִּק D 2:40, 44, תַּדִּקִנַּהּ "(the kingdom) will crush it (the earth)" D 7:23, infinitive לְהַעָלָה, לְהַנְעָלָה, participle מְהַדֵּק, מַדֱּקָה, מַדֲּקָה. For the passive, cf. הֻעַל (*huʿʿal*) "he was brought in" D 5:13, הֻעַלוּ (*huʿʿálū*, possibly הֻעָלוּ, but not הַעֲלוּ) D 5:15.

## 12. Some special irregular verbs

**165.** Many roots combine two of the afore-mentioned irregularities. They have been mentioned under the one or the other, or both, relevant categories before.

**166.** Šap̄ʿe̩l formations: In addition to שכלל (par. 157) and
מְסוֹבְלִין (par. 130), BA has two more šap̄ʿe̩l formations borrowed *11*
from Akkadian, (א)שֵׁיצִי "to complete" (root *wḏʾ*) and שֵׁיזִב "to save" (root *ʿzb*) (יְשֵׁיזִב, יְשֵׁיזְבִנַּהּ, יְשֵׁיזְבִנְכוֹן, מְשֵׁיזִב, לְשֵׁיזָבוּתֵהּ).

**167.** אֲתָה "to come" has the hap̄ʿel הַיְתִי, הַיְתִיו, לְהַיְתָיָה, passive הֵיתָיִת (fem.) D 6:18, הֵיתָיו D 3:13.

**168.** הֲוָה "to be" uses forms of the imperfect with a preformative ל instead of the usual י: לֶהֱוֵא, לֶהֱוֹן, לֶהֶוְיָן.

**169.** *הלך "to go" is represented by participles of the paʿʿel and the hap̄ʿel, מְהַלֵּךְ, מַהְלְכִין (to be corrected to מְהַלְּכִין?). The imperfect and infinitive pᵊʿal are formed from a different root, *hwk*: יְהָךְ, לִמְהָךְ.

**170.** *חֲיָה "to live" has the hap̄ʿel **haḥḥī*, part. מַחֵא (*maḥḥē*) D 5:19.

**171.** כהל, יכל "to be able to, prevail": כהל forms the participle כָּהֵל, כָּהֲלִין. יכל has the perfect יְכִל, יְכֵלְתָּ, the participle יָכִל, יָכְלָה, יָכְלִין, the imperfect יִכֻּל, יוּכַל, תּוּכַל (*tūḵal*, read *tikkul*). For *yikkul*, cf. par. 128; *yūḵal*, probably an ancient hup̄ʿal formation, is commonly used in Hebrew and preserved here in BA.

As in English, כהל, יכל are followed by the infinitive introduced by ל.

**172.** *סְלִק "to go up." In forms in which סל are not separated by a vowel, ל is assimilated to ס. The resulting *ss* may be nasalized: pᵊʿal סִלְקַת (rather than סִלְקָת D 7:8), סְלִקוּ, סָלְקָן, but hap̄ʿel הַסִּקוּ, לְהַנְסָקָה, passive הֻסַּק.

**173.** *אִשְׁתִּי "to drink" shows prothetic *ʾi-* only in the perfect; cf. the participle שָׁתֵה, שָׁתַיִן, imperfect יִשְׁתּוֹן.

## 13. The verb with pronominal suffixes

For a listing of all attested forms, cf. the paradigms, p. 75.

**174.** The forms of the verbal suffixes are the same as those of the noun (par. 31), except for the suffix of the 1. sg. which is ־נִי (unstressed). This ־נִי is used also with the infinitive: לְהוֹדָעוּתַנִי "to let me know."

There is no pronominal suffix for the 3. pl., but the seemingly independent personal pronoun הִמּוֹ, הִמּוֹן is used (par. 29).

**175.** In the imperfect, the suffix is preceded by *-(i)nn-*: יְהוֹדְעִנַּנִי "he will let me know," יְשֵׁיזְבִנָּךְ "he will save you," יִתְּנִנַּהּ "he gives it (fem.)." Reduction of *nn* > *n* occurs when it is vowelless: יְשְׁאֲלִנְכוֹן "he will ask you (pl.)" E 7:21, יְשֵׁיזְבִנְכוֹן "he will save you" D 3:15. In the 3. and 2. masc. pl., *-ūn-n* was perhaps pronounced *-unn-*, with shortened *u* (par. 10, 147).

In the jussive and the imperative, the suffix is attached directly to the verb: (-לוּךְ) אַל יְבַהֲלָךְ "let it (them) not frighten you!," הַעֲלְנִי "let me enter!"

**176.** Slightly different forms result when the suffixes are attached to roots ending in *w*/*y*/ʾ, such as יְחַוִּנַּהּ "he will tell it (fem.)" D 2:11.

## 14. Notes on the syntax of the verb

**177.** The participle may indicate the immediate present, for instance: מְהוֹדְעִין אֲנַחְנָה לְמַלְכָּא "we (hereby) inform the king" E 4:16.

This led to the widespread use of the participle to indicate an action that is simultaneous with the main action. Therefore, the participle must often be translated by the past tense, for instance: בַּהּ שַׁעֲתָה נְפַקָה אֶצְבְּעָן ... וְכָתְבָן "at this very moment, fingers ... came out and wrote" D 5:5.

This led further to the free use of the participle as a narrative tense, for instance: בֵּאדַיִן מִתְכַּנְּשִׁין אֲחַשְׁדַּרְפְּנַיָּא ··· וְקָיְמִין ··· וְכָרוֹזָא קָרֵא "thereupon, the satraps ... assembled ... and stood ... and the herald called" D 3:3f.

The participle may also be used to indicate continuous and habitual action, for instance: דִּי קִרְיְתָא דָךְ מִן יוֹמָת עָלְמָא עַל מַלְכִין מִתְנַשְּׂאָה וּמְרַד וְאֶשְׁתַּדּוּר מִתְעֲבֶד־בַּהּ "that this city has been rising up against kings since the days of eternity and rebellion and insurrection have (always) occurred in it" E 4:19. However, this mode is more commonly expressed by הֲוָה "to be" with the participle: וַהֲוָת בָּטְלָא "(work on the temple) was idle (all the time)" E 4:24, הֲוָה בְנֵה מִקַּדְמַת דְּנָה שְׁנִין שַׂגִּיאָן "(the temple) had been standing built formerly for many years" E 5:11, כָּל קֳבֵל דִּי הֲוָא עָבֵד מִן קַדְמַת דְּנָה "as he used to do formerly" D 6:11.

**178.** Use of the imperfect to indicate simultaneous action antedates that of the participle. In BA, it occurs rarely: עַיְנַי לִשְׁמַיָּא נִטְלֵת וּמַנְדְּעִי עֲלַי יְתוּב "I lifted my eyes toward heaven, and my knowledge returned to me" D 4:31.

The imperfect indicates the past after the conjunction "until" in E 5:5, עַד טַעְמָא לְדָרְיָוֶשׁ יְהָךְ "until Darius' order came."

The unexplained (וְאֻשַּׁיָּא) יַחִיטוּ E 4:12 is occasionally considered an imperfect (jussive?), but it would seem to be a perfect (*yaḥḥīṭū*, root *yḥṭ* < *wḥṭ* = *ḥwṭ* "they have walled the foundations," a gloss to the preceding וְשׁוּרַיָּא שַׁכְלִלוּ).

**179.** The perfect is used to indicate the future in D 7:27, וּמַלְכוּתָה ··· יְהִיבַת לְעַם קַדִּישֵׁי עֶלְיוֹנִין "the kingdom ... will be given to the people of the holy ones of the Most High." This may be due to the fact that the passive p$^{ə}$ʿal was felt to be closely related to the passive participle.

**180.** The verb of more than one subject may be either sg. or pl., regardless of whether it comes before or after the subjects.

**181.** The 3. masc. pl. and the masc. pl. of the participle frequently express an impersonal subject and thus substitute for a passive construction: וְלָךְ טָרְדִין מִן אֲנָשָׁא ··· וְעִשְׂבָּא כְתוֹרִין לָךְ יְטַעֲמוּן "they (one) will drive you out from mankind ... and will make you eat grass like oxen" = "you will be driven out, etc." D 4:22.

**182.** The direct object is frequently introduced by the preposition לְ. It may, however, be noted that in BA, a large percentage of these cases concerns the direct object of an infinitive or participle.

**183.** The position of words in a verbal sentence is free and does not follow any hard and fast rules. The more ancient sequence *verb-subject-object* occurs occasionally, in particular in dependent clauses and after such particles as כְּעַן "now," בֵּאדַיִן "then." Preference is shown to the sequence *object-verb-subject*. In sentences containing no direct object, the preferred sequence is *subject-verb*. Other combinations are possible.

**184.** The direct object may precede the verb and later in the sentence be referred to by the appropriate pronoun or pronominal suffix: וּבַיְתָה דְנָה סַתְרֵהּ וְעַמָּה הַגְלִי "and he tore down this house and exiled the people" E 5:12, הִמּוֹ (rather *ʾaḥḥeṯ*) אֵלֶּה מָאנַיָּא שֵׂא אֵזֶל אֲחֵת "take these vessels and go and deposit them" E 5:15 (contrast וְאַף מָאנֵי בֵית אֱלָהָא ··· יַהֲתִיבוּן E 6:5), גֻּבְרַיָּא אִלֵּךְ ··· קַטִּל הִמּוֹן שְׁבִיבָא דִּי נוּרָא "a fiery flame killed those men" D 3:22, וּשְׁאָר חֵיוָתָא הֶעְדִּיו

שָׁלְטָנְהוֹן "and they took away the dominion of all the other animals" D 7:12.

**185.** The infinitive may follow or precede its object. Examples of both usages occur with about equal frequency.

## XIV. The Vocabulary

**186.** Aramaic has been influenced to an extraordinary degree by the fact that it had to live together with—and was dominated by—a variety of other languages. Its vocabulary shows manifold layers of foreign influence which shed light upon the historical development of the language.

Inner-Aramaic preferences in the choice of words, for dialectal or stylistic reasons, can be observed in BA in the form of glosses that have entered the text: בְּדִתְאָא דִּי בָרָא for בַּעֲשַׂב אַרְעָא "with the vegetation of the field (earth)" D 4:12 (cf. Gen. 1:11f.), בְּנָגְהָא for בִּשְׁפַרְפָּרָא "at dawn" D 6:20.

A number of Hebrew, Akkadian, and Persian proper names of persons and localities are to be found in BA.

**187.** Hebrew influence must be assumed for many words of religious significance or words designating Jewish institutions. These may be completely aramaicized and may originally have been common to Aramaic and the Canaanite/Hebrew group, but their existence in BA is due to Jewish influence. Such words are נְבִיאָה "prophet," נְבוּאָה "prophecy," כָּהֲנַיָּא "priests," לֵוָיֵא "Levites," נְתִינַיָּא "temple servants," מִנְחָה "offering," נִיחוֹחִין "sacrifices of sweet smell," נִסְכֵּיהוֹן "their libations," מַלְאַךְ "angel," שִׁבְטֵי יִשְׂרָאֵל "the tribes of Israel" E 6:17, לְחַטָּיָא "to make a sin offering" E 6:17, חַרְטֹם "magician" (of Egyptian origin?). The fact of Hebrew origin is occasionally proven or made likely by phonetic reasons, as in שָׁפְטִין "judges" (par. 18) or עֶלְיוֹנִין "most high" (par. 22).

**188.** Akkadian influence extended over many centuries and also 16
reflects dialectal distinctions. There are ancient cultural loans, such as הֵיכְלָא "temple, palace" (< *ekallu*, through Hurrian and Canaanite?), כָּרְסֵא "chair" (< *kussium*, *kussū*), probably also אַתּוּן "furnace" (< *atūnu*). Terms such as אַרְגְּוָנָא "purple" (< *argamannu*) and פַּרְזֶל "iron" (< *parzillu*) entered Aramaic through Akkadian.

The bulk of Akkadian loan words concerns terms of the political and financial administration, such as סְגַן "prefect" (< *šaknu*), פֶּחָה "governor" (< *piḫatu, pāḫatu*), (*כְּנָת) *כְּנָה "colleague" (< *kinattu*), (מִנְדָּה) מִדָּה, בְּלוֹ, הֲלָךְ for various kinds of taxes (< *ma(n)dattu, biltu, ilku*), נִכְסִין "possessions" (< pl. *nik(k)assū*), אִגְּרָה "letter" (< *egirtu*). Terms for monetary units such as מְנֵא "mina" (< *manū*) and פְּרֵס "half-mina" or "half-shekel" (< *parsu*) are derived from Akkadian. There are loan translations such as תַּלְתָּא "triumvir" (< *šalšu*, par. 71), עֲבַר נַהֲרָא "the Trans-Euphrates Province" (lit., "across-the-river," < *eber nāri*), בְּעֵל טְעֵם "official in charge" (< *bēl ṭēmi*).

Military influence is indicated in בִּירְתָא "fortress" (< *bīrtu*) and, possibly, קְרָב "war" (< *qarābu*?). A legal loan word is זָכוּ "innocence" (< *zakūtu*).

Another group of Akkadian loan words are cultural terms connected with architecture (נִדְבָּךְ "layer" < *nadbaku*, and, possibly,
11 מְסוֹבְלִין [par. 130] < imp. *šūbil*); with palace life (שֵׁגְלָתָא "concubines" < **ša ekalli*?); and religious practices (אָשַׁף "enchanter" < *āšipu*).

Finally, there are ordinary words, such as the verbs שֵׁיזִב "to save" (< *ušēzib*), (א)שֵׁיצִי "to complete" (< *ušēṣī*), שַׁכְלֵל "to complete" (< *ušaklil*), possibly also חשח "needed, necessary" (from the root *ḫašāḫu*); further, זִיו "facial features" (< pl. *zīmū*). Their acceptance attests to the intimate contact between the two languages.

**189.** Persian influence shows itself in the sphere of political and legal administration and in the phraseology of written communication. Thus, we find אֲחַשְׁדַּרְפְּנַיָּא "satraps" (< **xšaϑrapāna*, through Akkadian?; OPers. has a different formation, *xšaśapāvā*, and the Greek form presupposes **xšaϑrapā*), אֲדַרְגָּזְרַיָּא "counselors" (?, < **handarza-kara*, Mod. Pers. *andarzġar*), הַדָּבְרִין "companions" (< **hada-bāra*, MPers. *hadbār*, Mod. Pers. *yār*), סָרְכִין "chief ministers" (< **sāraka*, to Av. *sāra* "head"), גִּזַּבְרַיָּא, גְּדָבְרַיָּא "treasurers," גִּנְזַיָּא "treasures" (< *ganzabara, ganza*, Mod. Pers. *ganjūr, ganj*), אֲפַרְסַתְכָיֵא "leading officials" (?, < **fra-stā-ka*, corresponding to Greek *prostatēs*?, or to be corrected to אֲפַרְסְכָיֵא < **frasaka* > Akkad. *ip-ra-sak-ka*?), תִּפְתָּיֵא "police chiefs" (< **tāyu-pātā*), דְּתָבְרַיָּא "law officials," דָּת "law" (< *dātabara, dāta*, Mod. Pers. *dāvar, dād*),

שְׁרֹשִׁי "corporal punishment" (par. 19, 57, < *sraušyā, Av. sraošyā),
הַדָּמִין "limbs" (< *handāma(n), Mod. Pers. andām) in the legal
phrase הַדָּמִין תִּתְעַבְדוּן "you will be dismembered," נִשְׁתְּוָנָא "written
order" (< *ni-šta-van, Ossetic nystwan), פַּרְשֶׁגֶן "copy" (פִּתְשֶׁגֶן in a
Hebrew context, < *pati-čagna, Armen. patčēn, Pahl. pačēn),
פִּתְגָם "message, word" (< *pati-gāma, Mod. Pers. paygām). Cf. also
the loan translation מֶלֶךְ מַלְכַיָּא "king of kings." Epistolary and
documentary style also added some adverbs to the language, such
as אָסְפַּרְנָא "exactly, perfectly" (< *aspṛnā, Av. aspərənah), אַדְרַזְדָא
"diligently" (< *drazdā, Av. zrazdā). Cf. also אָזְדָא "publicly
known" (< azdā).

Cultural terms are represented by words used for various parts of
dress: המונכא "necklace" (qᵊrē הַמְנִיכָא, *הַמְיָנַכָּא < *hamyā(ha)na-
ka, Mod. Pers. hamyān "belt"), סַרְבָּלֵיהוֹן "their trousers" (< *sala-
vāra, Mod. Pers. šalvār), probably also פַּטִּישֵׁיהוֹן "their shirts" (?)
and כַּרְבְּלָתְהוֹן "their hats" (< Akk. karballatu, probably neither a
Persian nor an Akkadian word, but a part of Persian dress). A much
discussed building term, אֻשַּׁרְנָא "furnishings" (?, < āčarna, MPers.
āčār), also appears to be of Persian origin.

Ordinary words, such as רָזָא "secret" (< *rāza, Mod. Pers. rāz)
and * זַן "kind" (< zana), also found their way from Persian into
Aramaic.

190. A number of words may be suspected of being of Akkadian
or Persian origin. אַפְתֹם may be Akk. appittimma and mean "certainly," or Persian *apatama(m), MPers. abdum "finally." Further,
אֶשְׁתַּדּוּר "insurrection" (< Pers. *ā(x)šti-drauga "breach of peace,"
cf. par. 111), נְוָלִי (-לוּ) "dunghill" (Akk.?), נְבִזְבָּה "gift" (par. 62),
נִבְרַשְׁתָּא "lamp" (perhaps < Pers. *ni-brāšti-, to Av. brāz-, San-
skrit bhrāj- "to shine"), נִדְנֶה, probably to be read נִדְנַהּ "its sheath"
D 7:15 (< Pers. nidāni "container," in Elamite "storehouse;" cf.
nidāman, Mod. Pers. niyām "sheath").

191. Greek loan words belong to the cultural sphere. They are
the terms for musical instruments repeatedly mentioned in Daniel
ch. 3: קַיתְרֹ(וֹ)ס (qatrōs) "kitharis," פְּסַנְתֵּרִין (D 3:7) פְּסַנְטֵרִין "psaltē-
ri(o)n," סִיפֹנְיָה, סוּמְפֹּנְיָה "symphōnia." Greek origin has been claimed
but never been proved for other words. It also remains doubtful
whether טַרְפְּלָיֵא E 4:9 may mean "men from Tripolis."

# Paradigms

## 1. The strong verb

| Perfect | pəʿal | paʿʿẹl | hap̄ʿẹl |
|---|---|---|---|
| sg. 3. masc. | כְּתַב | כַּתֵּב (כַּתִּב) | הַכְתֵּב (אַכְתֵּב ,-תִּב) |
| 3. fem. | כִּתְבַת | כַּתְּבַת | הַכְתְּבַת |
| 2. masc. | כְּתַבְתְּ (כְּתַבְתָּ ,-תָּה) | כַּתֵּבְתְּ | הַכְתֵּבְתְּ |
| 2. fem. | כְּתַבְתִּי | כַּתֵּבְתִּי | הַכְתֵּבְתִּי |
| 1. | כִּתְבֵת | כַּתְּבֵת | הַכְתְּבֵת |
| pl. 3. masc. | כְּתַבוּ | כַּתִּבוּ | הַכְתִּבוּ |
| 3. fem. | כְּתַבָה (כתבו *kəṯīḇ*) | כַּתִּבָה | הַכְתִּבָה |
| 2. masc. | כְּתַבְתּוּן | כַּתֵּבְתּוּן | הַכְתֵּבְתּוּן |
| 2. fem. | כְּתַבְתֵּן | כַּתֵּבְתֵּן | הַכְתֵּבְתֵּן |
| 1. | כְּתַבְנָא | כַּתֵּבְנָא | הַכְתֵּבְנָא |

| Imperfect | | | |
|---|---|---|---|
| sg. 3. masc. | יִכְתֻּב | יְכַתֵּב (-תִּב) | יְהַכְתֵּב (יַכְתֵּב ,-תִּב) |
| 3. fem. | תִּכְתֻּב | תְּכַתֵּב | תְּהַכְתֵּב |
| 2. masc. | תִּכְתֻּב | תְּכַתֵּב | תְּהַכְתֵּב |
| 2. fem. | תִּכְתְּבִין | תְּכַתְּבִין | תְּהַכְתְּבִין |
| 1. | אֶכְתֻּב | אֲכַתֵּב | אֲהַכְתֵּב |
| pl. 3. masc. | יִכְתְּבוּן | יְכַתְּבוּן | יְהַכְתְּבוּן |
| 3. fem. | יִכְתְּבָן | יְכַתְּבָן | יְהַכְתְּבָן |
| 2. masc. | תִּכְתְּבוּן | תְּכַתְּבוּן | תְּהַכְתְּבוּן |
| 2. fem. | תִּכְתְּבָן | תְּכַתְּבָן | תְּהַכְתְּבָן |
| 1. | נִכְתֻּב | נְכַתֵּב | נְהַכְתֵּב |

| Imperative | pəʿal | paʿʿẹl | hap̄ʿẹl |
|---|---|---|---|
| sg. 2. masc. | כְּתֻב | כַּתֵּב (-תִּב) | הַכְתֵּב (אַכְתֵּב ,-תִּב) |
| 2. fem. | כְּתֻבִי | כַּתִּבִי | הַכְתִּבִי |
| pl. 2. masc. | כְּתֻבוּ | כַּתִּבוּ | הַכְתִּבוּ |
| 2. fem. | כְּתֻבָה | כַּתִּבָה | הַכְתִּבָה |

| Infinitive | pəʿal | paʿʿẹl | hap̄ʿẹl |
|---|---|---|---|
| | מִכְתַּב | כַּתָּבָה | הַכְתָּבָה (אַכְ-) |

| Participle | pəʿal act. | pəʿal pass. | paʿʿẹl act. | paʿʿẹl pass. |
|---|---|---|---|---|
| sg. masc. | כָּתֵב (כָּתִב) | כְּתִיב | מְכַתֵּב (-תִּב) | מְכַתַּב |
| fem. | כָּתְבָה | כְּתִיבָה | מְכַתְּבָה | מְכַתְּבָה |
| pl. masc. | כָּתְבִין | כְּתִיבִין | מְכַתְּבִין | מְכַתְּבִין |
| fem. | כָּתְבָן | כְּתִיבָן | מְכַתְּבָן | מְכַתְּבָן |

| | hap̄ʿẹl act. | hap̄ʿẹl pass. |
|---|---|---|
| sg. masc. | מְהַכְתֵּב (מַכְתֵּב ,-תִּב) | מְהַכְתַּב |
| fem. | מְהַכְתְּבָה | מְהַכְתְּבָה |
| pl. masc. | מְהַכְתְּבִין | מְהַכְתְּבִין |
| fem. | מְהַכְתְּבָן | מְהַכְתְּבָן |

| Passive Perfect | pᵊʿīl | puʿʿal | hu/op̄ʿal |
|---|---|---|---|
| sg. 3. masc. | כְּתִיב | כֻּתַּב | הֻכְתַּב (הָכְ-) |
| 3. fem. | כְּתִיבַת | כֻּתְּבַת | הֻכְתְּבַת |
| 2. masc. | כְּתִיבְתְּ (-תָּה) | כֻּתַּבְתְּ | הֻכְתַּבְתְּ |
| 2. fem. | כְּתִיבְתִּי | כֻּתַּבְתִּי | הֻכְתַּבְתִּי |
| 1. | כְּתִיבֵת | כֻּתְּבֵת | הֻכְתְּבֵת |
| pl. 3. masc. | כְּתִיבוּ | כֻּתַּבוּ | הֻכְתַּבוּ |
| 3. fem. | כְּתִיבָה | כֻּתַּבָה | הֻכְתַּבָה |
| 2. masc. | כְּתִיבְתּוּן | כֻּתַּבְתּוּן | הֻכְתַּבְתּוּן |
| 2. fem. | כְּתִיבְתֵּן | כֻּתַּבְתֵּן | הֻכְתַּבְתֵּן |
| 1. | כְּתִיבְנָא | כֻּתַּבְנָא | הֻכְתַּבְנָא |

| Perfect | hiṯpᵊʿẹl | hiṯpaʿʿal |
|---|---|---|
| sg. 3. masc. | הִתְכְּתֵב (אֶתְ-, -תִּב) | הִתְכַּתַּב (אֶתְ-) |
| 3. fem. | הִתְכַּתְבַת | הִתְכַּתְּבַת |
| 2. masc. | הִתְכְּתֵבְתְּ (-תֵּבְתָּ) | הִתְכַּתַּבְתְּ |
| 2. fem. | הִתְכְּתֵבְתִּי | הִתְכַּתַּבְתִּי |
| 1. | הִתְכַּתְבֵת | הִתְכַּתְּבֵת |
| pl. 3. masc. | הִתְכְּתִבוּ | הִתְכַּתַּבוּ |
| 3. fem. | הִתְכְּתִבָה | הִתְכַּתַּבָה |
| 2. masc. | הִתְכְּתֵבְתּוּן | הִתְכַּתַּבְתּוּן |
| 2. fem. | הִתְכְּתֵבְתֵּן | הִתְכַּתַּבְתֵּן |
| 1. | הִתְכְּתֵבְנָא | הִתְכַּתַּבְנָא |

*even though Dagesh doubles letters, we is to put a stop on pronunciation*

| Imperfect | hiṯp<sup></sup>ᵉʿẹl | hiṯpaʿʿal |
|---|---|---|
| sg. 3. masc. | יִתְכְּתֵב (-תִב) | יִתְכַּתַּב |
| 3. fem. | תִּתְכְּתֵב | תִּתְכַּתַּב |
| 2. masc. | תִּתְכְּתֵב | תִּתְכַּתַּב |
| 2. fem. | תִּתְכַּתְבִין | תִּתְכַּתְּבִין |
| 1. | אֶתְכְּתֵב | אֶתְכַּתַּב |
| pl. 3. masc. | יִתְכַּתְבוּן | יִתְכַּתְּבוּן |
| 3. fem. | יִתְכַּתְבָן | יִתְכַּתְּבָן |
| 2. masc. | תִּתְכַּתְבוּן | תִּתְכַּתְּבוּן |
| 2. fem. | תִּתְכַּתְבָן | תִּתְכַּתְּבָן |
| 1. | נִתְכְּתֵב | נִתְכַּתַּב |

| Infinitive | | |
|---|---|---|
| | הִתְכְּתָבָה (אֶתְ-) | הִתְכַּתָּבָה (אֶתְ-) |

| Participle | | |
|---|---|---|
| sg. masc. | מִתְכְּתֵב (-תִב) | מִתְכַּתַּב |
| fem. | מִתְכַּתְבָה | מִתְכַּתְּבָה |
| pl. masc. | מִתְכַּתְבִין | מִתְכַּתְּבִין |
| fem. | מִתְכַּתְבָן | מִתְכַּתְּבָן |

## 2. Roots with ו or י as the second consonant

| Perfect | pᵊʿal | hap̄ʿel | hitpᵊʿel |
|---|---|---|---|
| sg. 3. masc. | קָם (שָׂם, רִם) | הֲקִים (הֲקֵים, אֲקִים) | |
| 3. fem. | קָמַת | הֲקִימַת | |
| 2. masc. | קָמְתָּ | הֲקֵימְתָּ | |
| 2. fem. | קָמְתִּי | הֲקֵימְתִּי | |
| 1. | קָמֶת | הֲקֵימֶת | |
| pl. 3. masc. | קָמוּ | הֲקִימוּ | |
| 3. fem. | קָמָה | הֲקִימָה | |
| 2. masc. | קָמְתּוּן | הֲקֵימְתּוּן | |
| 2. fem. | קָמְתֵּן | הֲקֵימְתֵּן | |
| 1. | קָמְנָא | הֲקֵימְנָא | |

| Imperfect | pᵊʿal | hap̄ʿel | hitpᵊʿel |
|---|---|---|---|
| sg. 3. masc. | יְקוּם (יְשִׂים) | יְקִים, יְהָקֵים | יִתְּזִין, יִתְּשָׂם |
| 3. fem. | תְּקוּם | תְּקִים (תָּסֵיף) | |
| 2. masc. | תְּקוּם | תְּקִים | |
| 2. fem. | תְּקוּמִין | תְּקִימִין | |
| 1. | אֲקוּם | אֲקִים | |
| pl. 3. masc. | יְקוּמוּן | יְקִימוּן (יַהֲקִימוּן) | יִתְּשָׂמוּן |
| 3. fem. | יְקוּמָן | יְקִימָן | |
| 2. masc. | תְּקוּמוּן | תְּקִימוּן | |
| 2. fem. | תְּקוּמָן | תְּקִימָן | |
| 1. | נְקוּם | נְקִים | |

| Imperative | pəʿal | hap̄ʿel | hitp̱əʿel |
|---|---|---|---|
| sg. 2. masc. | קוּם (שִׂים) | הֲקִים | |
| 2. fem. | קֻוּמִי (שִׂימִי) | הֲקִימִי | |
| pl. 2. masc. | קוּמוּ (שִׂימוּ) | הֲקִימוּ | |
| 2. fem. | קוּמָה (שִׂימָה) | הֲקִימָה | |

| Infinitive | | |
|---|---|---|
| מְקָם | הֲקָמָה | הִתְּשָׂמָה |

| Participle | act. | pass. | act. | pass. | |
|---|---|---|---|---|---|
| sg. masc. | קָאֵם | שִׂים | מְהָקֵים (מָקִים, מְקִים) | מְקָם (?) | מִתְּשָׂם |
| fem. | קָיְמָה (קאמה) | שִׂימָה | מְקִימָה | | מִתְּשָׂמָה |
| pl. masc. | קָיְמִין (קאמין) | שִׂימִין | מְקִימִין | | מִתְּשָׂמִין |
| fem. | קָיְמָן (קאמן) | שִׂימָן | מְקִימָן | | מִתְּשָׂמָן |

| Passive Perfect | pəʿīl | hu/op̄ʿal |
|---|---|---|
| sg. 3. masc. | שִׂים (?) | |
| 3. fem. | שָׂמַת | הֲקִימַת (הֳקָמַת?) |

### 3. Roots ending in ו/י or א

| Perfect | pəʿal | | paʿʿẹl | hap̄ʿẹl |
|---|---|---|---|---|
| sg. 3. masc. | בְּנָה | (אִשְׁתִּי) | בַּנִּי | הַבְנִי |
| 3. fem. | בְּנָת | (אִשְׁתִּיַת ?) | בַּנִּיַת (?) | הַבְנִיַת (?) |
| 2. masc. | בְּנַיְתָ | (אִשְׁתִּיתָ) | בַּנִּיתָ | הַבְנִיתָ |
| 2. fem. | בְּנַיְתִי | (אִשְׁתִּיתִי) | בַּנִּיתִי | הַבְנִיתִי |
| 1. | בְּנֵית | (אִשְׁתִּית) | בַּנִּית | הַבְנִית |
| pl. 3. masc. | בְּנוֹ | (אִשְׁתִּיו) | בַּנִּיו | הַבְנִיו |
| 3. fem. | בְּנָה (?) | (אִשְׁתִּיָּה ?) | בַּנִּיָּה (?) | הַבְנִיָּה (?) |
| 2. masc. | בְּנֵיתוֹן | (אִשְׁתִּיתוֹן) | בַּנִּיתוֹן | הַבְנִיתוֹן |
| 2. fem. | בְּנֵיתֵן | (אִשְׁתִּיתֵן) | בַּנִּיתֵן | הַבְנִיתֵן |
| 1. | בְּנֵינָא | (אִשְׁתִּינָא) | בַּנִּינָא | הַבְנִינָא |

| Imperfect | | | |
|---|---|---|---|
| sg. 3. masc. | יִבְנֵא | יְבַנֵּא | יְהַבְנֵא (יַבְנֵא) |
| 3. fem. | תִּבְנֵא | תְּבַנֵּא | תְּהַבְנֵא |
| 2. masc. | תִּבְנֵא | תְּבַנֵּא | תְּהַבְנֵא |
| 2. fem. | תִּבְנֵין (?) | תְּבַנֵּין (?) | תְּהַבְנֵין (?) |
| 1. | אֶבְנֵא | אֲבַנֵּא | אֲהַבְנֵא |
| pl. 3. masc. | יִבְנוֹן | יְבַנּוֹן | יְהַבְנוֹן |
| 3. fem. | יִבְנְיָן | יְבַנְּיָן | יְהַבְנְיָן |
| 2. masc. | תִּבְנוֹן | תְּבַנּוֹן | תְּהַבְנוֹן |
| 2. fem. | תִּבְנְיָן | תְּבַנְּיָן | תְּהַבְנְיָן |
| 1. | נִבְנֵא | נְבַנֵּא | נְהַבְנֵא |

| Imperative | pᵊʿal | paʿʿẹl | hap̄ʿẹl |
|---|---|---|---|
| sg. 2. masc. | בְּנִי | בַּנִּי (מֶנִּי) | הַבְנִי |
| 2. fem. | | | |
| pl. 2. masc. | בְּנוֹ | בַּנּוֹ | הַבְנוֹ |
| 2. fem. | | | |
| | | | |
| Infinitive | מִבְנֵא | בַּנָּיָה | הַבְנָיָה |

| Participle | pᵊʿal | | paʿʿẹl | | hap̄ʿẹl | |
|---|---|---|---|---|---|---|
| | act. | pass. | act. | pass. | act. | pass. |
| sg. masc. | בָּנֵה (ـֵא) | בְּנֵה (ـֵא) | מְבַנֵּא | מְבַנַּי (!) | מְהַבְנֵא (מַבְנֵא) | מְהַבְנַי (!) |
| fem. | בָּנְיָה | בְּנָיָה | מְבַנְּיָה | מְבַנְּיָה | מְהַבְנְיָה | מְהַבְנְיָה |
| pl. masc. | בָּנַיִן | בְּנַיִן | מְבַנַּיִן | מְבַנַּיִן | מְהַבְנַיִן | מְהַבְנַיִן |
| fem. | בָּנְיָן | בְּנָיָן | מְבַנְּיָן | מְבַנְּיָן | מְהַבְנְיָן | מְהַבְנְיָן |

| Passive Perfect | | |
|---|---|---|
| sg. 3. masc. | בְּנִי | |
| 3. fem. | | הֵיתָיִת |
| pl. 3. masc. | בְּנִיו | הֵיתָיוּ |

| Perfect | hitp̱ᵊʿel | hitpaʿʿal |
|---|---|---|
| sg. 3. masc. | הִתְבְּנִי (אֶתְ-) | הִתְבַּנִּי (אֶתְ-) |
| 3. fem. | הִתְבְּנִיַת | הִתְבַּנִּיַת (?) |
| 2. masc. | הִתְבְּנִ֫יתָ | הִתְבַּנִּ֫יתָ |
| 2. fem. | הִתְבְּנִ֫יתִי | הִתְבַּנִּ֫יתִי |
| 1. | הִתְבְּנִית | הִתְבַּנִּית |
| pl. 3. masc. | הִתְבְּנִיו | הִתְבַּנִּיו |
| 3. fem. | הִתְבְּנִ֫יָּה (?) | הִתְבַּנִּ֫יָּה (?) |
| 2. masc. | הִתְבְּנִיתוּן | הִתְבַּנִּיתוּן |
| 2. fem. | הִתְבְּנִיתֵן | הִתְבַּנִּיתֵן |
| 1. | הִתְבְּנִ֫ינָא | הִתְבַּנִּ֫ינָא |

| Imperfect | | |
|---|---|---|
| sg. 3. masc. | יִתְבְּנֵא | יִתְבַּנֵּא |
| 3. fem. | תִּתְבְּנֵא | תִּתְבַּנֵּא |
| 2. masc. | תִּתְבְּנֵא | תִּתְבַּנֵּא |
| 2. fem. | תִּתְבְּנֵין (?) | תִּתְבַּנֵּין (?) |
| 1. | אֶתְבְּנֵא | אֶתְבַּנֵּא |
| pl. 3. masc. | יִתְבְּנוֹן | יִתְבַּנּוֹן |
| 3. fem. | יִתְבַּנְיָן | יִתְבַּנְּיָן |
| 2. masc. | תִּתְבְּנוֹן | תִּתְבַּנּוֹן |
| 2. fem. | תִּתְבַּנְיָן | תִּתְבַּנְּיָן |
| 1. | נִתְבְּנֵא | נִתְבַּנֵּא |

| Infinitive | הִתְבְּנָיָה | הִתְבַּנָּיָה |
|---|---|---|

| Participle | | |
|---|---|---|
| sg. masc. | מִתְבְּנֵא | מִתְבַּנֵּא |
| fem. | מִתְבַּנְיָה | מִתְבַּנְּיָה |
| pl. masc. | מִתְבַּנַ֫יִן | מִתְבַּנַּ֫יִן |
| fem. | מִתְבַּנְיָן | מִתְבַּנְּיָן |

## 4. Roots with identical second and third consonants

| Perfect | pᵊʿal | hap̄ʿẹl | hu/op̄ʿal |
|---|---|---|---|
| sg. 3. masc. | עַל | הַעֵל (הַנְעֵל ,אַ-) | הֻעַל |
| 3. fem. | עַלַלַת (נַדַּת) | הַעֶלֶת | |
| 2. masc. | עֲלַלְתָּ | הַעֵלְתָּ | |
| 2. fem. | עֲלַלְתִּי | הַעֵלְתִּי | |
| 1. | עַלַלֵת | הַעֶלֶת | |
| pl. 3. masc. | עַלּוּ | הַעִלּוּ | הֻעַלּוּ |
| 3. fem. | עַלָּה | הַעִלָּה | |
| 2. masc. | עֲלַלְתּוּן | הַעֵלְתּוּן | |
| 2. fem. | עֲלַלְתֵּן | הַעֵלְתֵּן | |
| 1. | עֲלַלְנָא | הַעֵלְנָא | |

| Imperfect | | |
|---|---|---|
| sg. 3. masc. | יֵעֹל | יְהַעֵל (יֵעֵל) |
| 3. fem. | תֵּעֹל | תְּהַעֵל |
| 2. masc. | תֵּעֹל | תְּהַעֵל |
| 2. fem. | תֵּעֳלִּין | תְּהַעֲלִּין |
| 1. | אֵעֹל | אֲהַעֵל |
| pl. 3. masc. | יֵעֳלּוּן | יְהַעֲלּוּן |
| 3. fem. | יֵעֳלָּן | יְהַעֲלָּן |
| 2. masc. | תֵּעֳלּוּן | תְּהַעֲלּוּן |
| 2. fem. | תֵּעֳלָּן | תְּהַעֲלָּן |
| 1. | נֵעֹל | נְהַעֵל |

| Imperative | pᵊʿal | hap̄ʿẹl |
|---|---|---|
| sg. 2. masc. | עֹל | הַעֵל (הַנְעֵל, אַ-) |
| 2. fem. | עֹ֫לִּי | הַעִ֫לִּי |
| pl. 2. masc. | עֹ֫לּוּ | הַעִ֫לּוּ |
| 2. fem. | עֹ֫לָּה | הַעִ֫לָּה |

| Infinitive | pᵊʿal | hap̄ʿẹl |
|---|---|---|
| | מֵעַל | הֶעָלָה (הַנְעָלָה) |

| Participle | pᵊʿal | | hap̄ʿẹl | |
|---|---|---|---|---|
| | act. | pass. | act. | pass. |
| sg. masc. | עָלֵל | עֲלִיל | מְהַעֵל (מַעֵל) | מְהַעַל (מַעַל) |
| fem. | עָלָלה | | מְהַעֲלָה | |
| pl. masc. | עָלְלִין | | מְהַעֲלִין | |
| fem. | עָלָלן | | מְהַעֲלָן | |

## 5. Verbs with pronominal suffixes

| | Perfect | | | | Imperative | |
|---|---|---|---|---|---|---|
| | sg. | | | pl. | sg. | pl. |
| | 3. masc. | 2. masc. | 1. | 3. masc. | 2. masc. | 2. masc. |
| suffix sg. 1. | | הוֹדַעְתַּנִי | | חַבְּלוּנִי | הַעֲלְנִי | הַחֲוֹנִי |
| 2. masc. | הוֹדְעָךְ<br>הַשְׁלְטָךְ | | | | | |
| 3. masc. | סַתְרֵהּ<br>שָׂמֵהּ שַׁכְלְלֵהּ<br>הַשְׁלְטֵהּ בְּנָהִי<br>הֲקִימֵהּ (אֲקִימֵהּ) | | | הַקְרְבוּהִי<br>שְׁנוֹהִי | | חַבְּלוּהִי |
| 3. fem. | חַתְמַהּ<br>הַשְׁלְמַהּ | | בְּנֵיתַהּ | | | |
| pl. 1. | | הוֹדַעְתֶּנָא | | הֱתִיבוּנָא | | |

### Imperfect

| | sg. | | | pl. | |
|---|---|---|---|---|---|
| | 3. masc. | 3. fem. | 1. | 3. masc. | 2. masc. |
| suffix sg. 1. | יְדַחֲלִנַּנִי<br>יְהוֹדְעִנַּנִי<br>יְחַוִּנַּנִי | | | יְהוֹדְעֻנַּנִי<br>יְבַהֲלוּנַּנִי (-לֻנַּנִי) | תְּהוֹדְעוּנַּנִי (-עֻנַּנִי)<br>תְּהַחֲוֻנַּנִי |
| 2. masc. | יְשֵׁיזְבִנָּךְ<br>(jussive) יְבַהֲלָךְ | | | (jussive) יְבַהֲלוּךְ | |
| 3. masc. | | | אֲהוֹדְעִנֵּהּ | יְשַׁמְשׁוּנֵּהּ<br>יְבַהֲלוּנֵּהּ (-לֻנֵּהּ)<br>יְטַעֲמוּנֵּהּ | |
| 3. fem. | יְתְנִנַּהּ<br>יְחַוִּנַּהּ | תְּדוּשִׁנַּהּ<br>תְּדָקִנַּהּ | | | |
| pl. 2. masc. | יְשָׁאֲלִנְּכוֹן<br>יְשֵׁיזְבִנְּכוֹן | | | | |

# Short Bibliography

## (a) General Studies in Aramaic

Beyer (K.), *Die aramäischen Texte vom Toten Meer* (Göttingen, 1984).

Blau (J.), *On Pseudo-Corrections in Some Semitic Languages* (Jerusalem, 1970).

Cohen (D.), *La phrase nominale et l'évolution du système verbal en Sémitique* (Paris 1984).

Degen (R.), *Altaramäische Grammatik* (Wiesbaden, 1969. *Abhandlungen für die Kunde des Morgenlandes*, XXXVIII, 3).

Donner (H.) and Rölling (W.), *Kanaanäische und aramäische Inschriften* (Wiesbaden, 1962—64, 3rd ed., 1971—76).

Fitzmyer (J. A.), *The Genesis Apocryphon*, 2nd ed. (Rome, 1971).

Fitzmyer (J. A.) and Harrington (D. J.), *A Manual of Palestinian Aramaic Texts* (Rome, 1978).

Fitzmyer (J. A.) and Kaufman (S. A.), *An Aramaic Bibliography. Part I* (Baltimore and London, 1992).

Garr (W. R.), *Dialect Geography of Syria-Palestine*, 1000—586 B. C. (Philadelphia, 1985).

Hug (V.), *Altaramäische Grammatik der Texte des 7. und 6. Jh.s v. Chr.* (Heidelberg, 1993. *Heidelberger Studien zum Alten Orient* IV).

Kaufman (S. A.), *The Akkadian Influences on Aramaic* (Chicago, 1974).

Kaufman (S. A.), *The History of Aramaic Vowel Reduction*, in Sokoloff (M.) (ed.), *Aramaeans, Aramaic and the Aramaic Literary Tradition*, 47—55 (Ramat Gan, 1983). See also idem, in *Journal of the American Oriental Society*, CIV (1984), 87—95.

Kutscher (E. Y.), *Aramaic*, in *Current Trends in Linguistics*, VI, 347—412 (The Hague, 1970).

Maraqten (M.), *Die semitischen Personennamen in den alt- und reichsaramäischen Inschriften aus Vorderasien* (Hildesheim, 1988).

Morag (S.), *The Vocalization Systems of Arabic, Hebrew, and Aramaic* (The Hague, 1962, 1972).

Muraoka (T.), *The Tell-Fekheriye Bilingual Inscription and Early Aramaic*, in *Abr-Nahrain*, XXII (1983—84), 79—117.

Naveh (J.), *The Development of the Aramaic Script* (Jerusalem, 1970. *Proceedings of the Israel Academy of Sciences and Humanities*, V, 1).

Rosenthal (F.), *Die aramaistische Forschung seit Th. Nöldeke's Veröffentlichungen* (Leiden, 1939).

Rosenthal (F.) (ed.), *An Aramaic Handbook* (Wiesbaden, 1967).

Segert (S.), *Altaramäische Grammatik* (Leipzig, 1975).

Soden (W. von), *Aramäische Wörter in neuassyrischen und neu- und spätbabylonischen Texten*, in *Orientalia, N. S.*, XXXV (1966), 1—20, XXXVII (1968), 261—271.

Teixidor (J.), *Bulletin d'épigraphie sémitique (1964—1980)* (Paris 1986).

Tropper (J.), *Die Inschriften von Zincirli* (Münster, 1993. *Abhandlungen zur Literatur Alt-Syrien-Palästinas*, VI).

Wagner (M.), *Die lexikalischen und grammatikalischen Aramaismen im alttestamentlichen Hebräisch* (Berlin, 1966. *Beihefte zur Zeitschrift für die Alttestamentliche Wissenschaft*, XCVI).

## (b) Studies and Commentaries on the Aramaic Texts of the Bible

Charles (R. H.), *A Critical and Exegetical Commentary on the Book of Daniel* (Oxford, 1929).

Delcor (M.), *Le livre de Daniel* (Paris, 1971).

Ginsberg (H. L.), *Studies in Daniel* (New York, 1948).

Hartman (L. F.) and Di Lella (A. A.), *The Book of Daniel* (Garden City, New York, 1978).

Jerusalmi (I.), *The Aramaic Sections of Ezra and Daniel* (Cincinnati, 1978).

Katz (R. G.), *Translatio Imperii. Untersuchungen zu den aramäischen Danielerzählungen und ihrem theologiegeschichtlichen Umfeld* (Neukirchen-Vluyn, 1991. *Wissenschaftliche Monographien zum Alten und Neuen Testament*, LXIII).

Mertens (A.), *Das Buch Daniel im Lichte der Texte vom Toten Meer* (Würzburg, 1971. *Stuttgarter Biblische Monographien*, XII).

Montgomery (J. A.), *The Book of Daniel* (New York, 1927).

Rudolph (W.), *Esra und Nehemia* (Tübingen, 1949).

Ulrich (E.), *Daniel Manuscripts from Qumran*, in *Bulletin of the American Schools of Oriental Research*, CCLXVIII (1987), 17—37; CCLXXIV (1989), 3—26.

## (c) BA Grammars and Grammatical Studies

Bauer (H.) and Leander (P.), *Grammatik des Biblisch-Aramäischen* (Halle, 1927). Also, *Kurzgefaßte Biblisch-Aramäische Grammatik* (Halle, 1929).

Blake (F. R.), *A Resurvey of Hebrew Tenses, with an appendix: Hebrew Influence on Biblical Aramaic* (Rome, 1951. *Scripta Pontificii Instituti Biblici*, CIII).

—, *Studies in Semitic Grammar V*, in *Journal of the American Oriental Society*, LXXIII (1953), 7—16.

Carmignac (J.), *Un aramaïsme biblique et qumrânien: L'infinitif placé après son complément d'objet*, in *Revue de Qumran*, V (1964—66), 503—520.

Cohen (D. R.), *Subject and Object in Biblical Aramaic* (Malibu, 1975. *Afroasiatic Linguistics*, II, 1).

Coxon (P. W.), *A Philological Note on 'štyw*, in *Zeitschrift für die Alttestamentliche Wissenschaft*, LXXXIX (1977), 275f.

Coxon (P. W.), *The Syntax of the Aramaic of Daniel*, in *Hebrew Union College Annual*, XLVIII (1977), 107—122.

Coxon (P. W.), *The Problem of Consonantal Mutations in Biblical Aramaic*, in *Zeitschrift der Deutschen Morgenländischen Gesellschaft*, CXXIX (1979), 8—22.

Fassberg (S. E.), *The Origin of the Ketib/Qere in the Aramaic Portions of Ezra and Daniel*, in *Vetus Testamentum* XXXIX (1989), 1—12. See also Morrow (D. S.) and Clarke (E. G.), in *Vetus Testamentum*, XXXVI (1986), 406—22.

Fitzmyer (J. A.), *The Syntax of kl, kl' in the Aramaic Texts from Egypt and in Biblical Aramaic*, in *Biblica*, XXXVIII (1957), 170—184, reprinted in idem, *A Wandering Aramaean*, 204—217 (Chico, CA, 1979).

Garr (W. R.), *On the Alternation between Construct and dī Phrases in Biblical Aramaic*, in *Journal of Semitic Studies*, XXXV (1990), 213—231.

Kaddari (M. Z.), *Construct State and dī-Phrases in Imperial Aramaic*, in *Proceedings of the International Conference on Semitic Studies*, Jerusalem 1965, 102—115 (Jerusalem, 1969).

Khan (G.), *Studies in Semitic Syntax* (Oxford, 1988).

Marti (K.), *Kurzgefasste Grammatik der Biblisch-Aramäischen Sprache* (Berlin, 1896, 1911, 1925. *Porta Linguarum Orientalium*).

Muraoka (T.), *Notes on the Syntax of Biblical Aramaic*, in *Journal of Semitic Studies*, XI (1966), 151—167.

Qimron (E.), *A Grammar of Biblical Aramaic* (in Hebrew) (Beer Sheva, 1990).

Schaeder (H. H.), *Iranische Beiträge* I, in *Schriften der Königsberger Gelehrten Gesellschaft, geisteswiss. Kl.*, VI (1930), 199—296.

Spitaler (A.), *Zur Frage der Konsonantendissimilation im Semitischen*, in *Indogermanische Forschungen*, LXI (1952—54), 257—266.

Strack (H. L.), *Grammatik des Biblisch-Aramäischen*, 6th ed. (Munich, 1921).

## (d) BA Dictionaries and Lexicographical Studies

Berger (P.-R.), *Zu den Namen Ššbṣr und Šn'ṣr*, in *Zeitschrift für die Alttestamentliche Wissenschaft*, LXXXIII (1971), 98—100. See also *Zeitschrift für Assyriologie*, LXIV (1975), 219—34.

Bowman (R. A.), *'eben g<sup>e</sup>lāl-aban galâlu*, in *Dōrōn: Hebraic Studies (Essays in Honor of A. I. Katsh)*, 64—74 (New York, 1965).

Cook (E. M.), *"In the plain of the wall" (Dan. 3:1)*, in *Journal of Biblical Literature*, CVIII (1989), 115f.

Eilers (W.), *Iranisches Beamtentum in der keilinschriftlichen Überlieferung*, in *Abhandlungen für die Kunde des Morgenlandes*, XXV (1940).

Ginsberg (H. L.), *Biblical Aramaic*, in Rosenthal (F.), *An Aramaic Handbook* (Wiesbaden, 1967), I/1, 17—39, I/2, 16—41.

Grelot (P.), *L'orchestre de Daniel*, in *Vetus Testamentum*, XXIX (1979), 26—38.

Hinz (W.), *Altiranisches Sprachgut der Nebenüberlieferungen* (Wiesbaden, 1975).

Koehler (L.) and Baumgartner (W.), *Lexicon in Veteris Testamenti Libros* (Leiden, 1948—53), 1045—1138 (Aramaic section by Baumgartner); *Supplementum* (Leiden, 1958), 195—208.

Mowinckel (S.), *Uššarnā*, in *Studia Theologica*, XIX (1965), 130—35.

Rundgren (F.), *Zur Bedeutung von šršw—Ezra VII, 26*, in *Vetus Testamentum*, VII (1957), 400—404.

Rundgren (F.), *Aramaica III: An Iranian Word in Daniel*, in *Orientalia Suecana*, XXV—XXVI (1976—77), 45—55 [on *'azdā*]; *Aramaica V: Biblical Aramaic 'adrazdā and śām bāl*, in *Orientalia Suecana*, XXXI—XXXII (1982—83), 143—46.

Shaffer (A.), *Hurrian *kirezzi, West Semitic krz*, in *Orientalia, N. S.*, XXXIV (1965), 32—34.

Sokoloff (M.), *ʿamar neqē* "Lamb's Wool,", in *Journal of Biblical Literature*, XCV (1976), 95.

Vogt (E.), *Lexicon linguae aramaicae Veteris Testamenti documentis antiquis illustratum* (Rome, 1971).

Williamson (H. G. M.), *'eben gĕlāl (Ezra 5:8, 6:4) again*, in *Bulletin of the American Schools of Oriental Research*, CCLXXX (1990), 83—88.

Wolters (A.), *Untying the King's Knots: Physiology and Wordplay in Daniel 5*, in *Journal of Biblical Literature*, CX (1991), 117—22.

Wolters (A.), *The Riddle of the Scales in Daniel 5*, in *Hebrew Union College Annual*, LXII (1991), 155—177.

## (e) Principal Editions of Aramaic Texts from Egypt[1]

Aimé-Giron (N.), *Adversaria Semitica*, in *Bulletin de l'Institut Français d'Archéologie Orientale*, XXXVIII (1939), 1—63.

[1] For papyri from the Achaemenid period found in Palestine, cf. Cross (F. M.), *Samaria Papyrus I*, in *Eretz-Israel*, XVIII (1985).

Bauer (H.) and Meissner (B.), *Ein aramäischer Pachtvertrag aus dem 7. Jahre Darius I.* (Berlin, 1936. *Sitzungsberichte d. Preuß. Akad. d. Wiss., phil.-hist. Kl.*).

Bresciani (E.), *Un papiro aramaico da El Hibeh del Museo Archeologico di Firenze*, in *Aegyptus*, XXXIX (1959), 3—8.

Bresciani (E.), *Papiri aramaici egiziani di epoca persiana presso il Museo Civico di Padova*, in *Rivista degli Studi Orientali*, XXXV (1960), 11—24.

Bresciani (E.), *Un papiro aramaico di età tolemaica*, in *Rendiconti, Accad. Naz. dei Lincei, Classe di scienze mor., stor. e filol.*, VIII, XVII, 5—6 (Rome, 1962), 258—264.

Bresciani (E.) and Kamil (M.), *Le lettere aramaiche di Hermopoli*, in *Atti* ..., VIII, XII, 5 (Rome, 1966), 359—428.

Cowley (A.), *Aramaic Papyri of the Fifth Century B. C.* (Oxford, 1923).

Degen (R.), *Ein neuer aramäischer Papyrus aus Elephantine*, in *Neue Ephemeris für Semitische Epigraphik*, I (1972), 9—22. Also, *Neue Ephemeris*, II (1974), 65—70, 71—78; *Neue Ephemeris*, III (1978), 15—31.

Driver (G. R.), *Aramaic Documents of the Fifth Century B. C.* (Oxford, 1954). Also, *Abridged and Revised Ed.* (Oxford, 1957).

Dupont-Sommer (A.), *Un papyrus araméen d'époque saïte découvert à Saqqarah*, in *Semitica*, I (1948), 43—68. Cf. Ginsberg (H. L.), in *Bulletin of the American Schools of Oriental Research*, CXL (1948), 24—27.

Grelot (P.), *Documents araméens d'Égypte* (Paris, 1972).

Kraeling (E. G.), *The Brooklyn Museum Papyri* (New Haven, 1953).

Porten (B.) and Yardeni (A.), *Textbook of Aramaic Documents from Ancient Egypt* (Jerusalem, 1986—).

Rabinowitz (I.), *Aramaic Inscriptions of the Fifth Century B. C. E. from a North-Arab Shrine in Egypt*, in *Journal of Near Eastern Studies*, XV (1956), 1—9, also XVIII (1959), 154f.

Segal (J. B.), *Aramaic Texts from North Saqqāra* (London, 1983).

## (f) Grammars and Dictionaries for the Texts from Egypt and Other Official Aramaic Material

Jean (C.-F.) and Hoftijzer (J.), *Dictionnaire des inscriptions sémitiques de l'Ouest* (Leiden, 1965).

Leander (P.), *Laut- und Formenlehre des Ägyptisch-Aramäischen* (Göteborg, 1928).

Vinnikov (I. N.), *Slovaŕ arameyskikh nadpisey*, in *Palestinskiy Sbornik*, III (66) (1958), 171—216, IV (67) (1959), 169—240, VII (70) (1962), 192—237, IX (72) (1962), 141—158, XI (74) (1963), 189—232, XIII (76) (1965), 217—262.

## Glossary

The numbers found after individual entries refer to the paragraphs where 18
a given root or word is cited. Italicized numbers indicate the more important occurrences.

In the abs. st. of some nouns, it is uncertain whether the last syllable had *a* or *ẹ*. In these cases, the last syllable is left unvocalized. In a very few other nouns, vowels are also omitted because of uncertainty as to their correct form.

Verbal roots are left entirely unvocalized. *ẹ/i* indicates the pᵉʿẹ/il. *Hitp.*, *pa.*, *hitpa.*, and *hap̄.* stand, respectively, for (h)itpᵉʿẹl, paʿʿẹl, (h)itpaʿʿal, and (h)ap̄ʿẹl. The distinction between *h* or the glottal stop as preformative has been disregarded.

* denotes merely that the *exact* form of a word thus marked does not occur in BA.

### א

| | |
|---|---|
| אַב* | father, *pl.* אֲבָהָן* (26, 49, *62*). |
| אֵב* | (*suff.* אִנְבֵּהּ) fruit. |
| אבד | to perish; *hap̄.* to destroy (26, *108*, *121*, *124*). |
| אֶ֫בֶן | stone (26, 46, *59*). |
| אִגְּרָה | (*det.* אִגַּרְתָּא) letter (46, 188). |
| אֱדַ֫יִן, בֵּאדַ֫יִן | then, thereupon (10, 13, 17, *75*, *85*, *89*, 177, 183). |
| אֲדָר | Adar (*month*) (74). |
| אִדַּר* | threshing floor. |
| אֲדַרְגָּזַר* | counselor (*189*). |
| אַדְרַזְדָּא | diligently (*93*, *189*). |
| אֶדְרָע | arm, might (17). |
| אַזְדָּא | publicly known, known as decided (86, *93*, *189*). |
| אזה | to heat (10, 13, 88, *121*, *123*, *149*). |
| אזל | to go (79, *122*, 184). |
| אַח* | brother, colleague (10, *62*). |
| אֲחִידָה* | riddle (111). |
| אַחְמְתָא | Ecbatana (*OPers. Hagmatāna*). |
| אַחֲרֵי | after (*prep.*) (*84*). |
| אַחֲרִי* | end (*57*). |
| אָחֳרִי | *see* אָחֳרָן. |
| אָחֳרֵין | (עַד ···) eventually (*89*). |

אָחֳרָן (*fem.* אָחֳרִי) other (10, *57*, *97*).
אֲחַשְׁדַּרְפַּן* satrap (177, *189*).
אִילָן tree.
אֵימְתָן* (*fem.* אֵימְתָנִי) frightful (15, *57*).
אִיתַי to exist, to be (49, 80, 86, *95*).
אכל to eat (26, *122*).
אַל not (*87*, 108, 152, 175).
אֵלה, אֵ֫לֶּה these (10, 26, *32*, *34*, 184).
אֱלָהּ god (13, 30, 36, 46—48, *49*, *75*, 80, 83, 84, *85*, 184).
אֱלוּ behold (*91*).
אִלֵּן, אִלֵּין these (*32*, *34*).
אִלֵּךְ those (*32*, 184).
אֲלַף thousand (42, *51*, *63*, *68*).
אַמָּה* (*pl.* אַמִּין) cubit (*61*).
אֻמָּה (*pl.* *אֻמִּין) nation (23, *61*).
אמן *hap̄.* (הֵימִן) to trust, *part. pass.* trusted, trustworthy (*124*).
אמר to say, to speak, to tell, to command (10, 13, 24, 27, *115*, *117*, *120*, *121*, *122*).
אִמַּר* lamb (79).
אִנְבֵּהּ *see* *אֵב.
אֲנָה I (26, *29*, 36, 88, 91).
אִנּוּן they, them, those (*29*, *30*, *32*, 38).
אֱנוֹשׁ* *see* אֱנָשׁ.
אֲנַ֫חְנָה, אֲנַ֫חְנָא we (26, *29*, 30, 177).
אִנִּין they (*fem.*) (*29*, *30*).
אנס to subdue, to be too difficult for.
אֲנַף* (*dual/pl.*) face.
אֱנָשׁ, אֱנוֹשׁ (*det.* אֲנָשָׁא) man, someone, men, mankind, human kind, people (*22*, 42, 181).
אַנְתְּה, אַנְתְּ you (*sg. masc.*) (*12*, *29*, 30, 36).
אַנְתָּה* (*pl. suff.* נְשֵׁיהוֹן) wife (*62*).
אַנְתּוּן you (*pl. masc.*) (*29*).
אֱסוּר fetter, (*pl.*) imprisonment (75, 86).
אָסְנַפַּר *to be corrected to* אס⟨רב⟩נפר Assurbanipal.
אָסְפַּ֫רְנָא exactly, perfectly (26, *93*, *189*).
אֱסָר interdict, prohibition.
אָע wood, timber, beam (*17*).

אַף also (*93*, 184).
אֲפָרְסָיֵא* Persian (?) *E 4:9*.
אֲפַרְסְכָיֵא* Persian (?) *E 5:6* (*189*).
אֲפַרְסַתְכָיֵא* magistrate (?) (*58*, *189*).
אָסְפַּרְנָא certainly *or* finally (*93*, *190*).
אֶצְבַּע* finger, toe (*59*, *60*, 177).
אַרְבַּע four (30, 59, *63*).
אַרְגְּוָן* purple (*188*).
אֲרוּ behold (*91*).
אֲרַח* (*pl.* *אֹרְחָן) way (10, *51*, *60*, 84).
אַרְיֵה (*pl.* *אַרְיָוָן) lion (48, *54*, 84).
אַרְיוֹךְ Arioch (*probably Persian*).
אֲרִיךְ proper (< *OPers. aryaka?*).
אַרְכֻבָּה* knee.
אַרְכָה (long) duration.
אַרְכְּוָיֵא* man from Uruk, Erechite.
אֲרַע* earth (17, *59*, 87, 186).
אֲרַעא lower, inferior (*adv.*) (80, *88*).
אַרְעִי* bottom (*57*).
אֲרַק* earth (*17*).
אַרְתַּחְשַׁשְׂתְּא (אַרְתַּחְשַׁסְתְּא) Artaxerxes (< *OPers. Artaxšaša, with Aramaic š/st for the peculiar OPers. š < ϑr*) (19, 79).
אֹשׁ* (pl. *אֻשִּׁין) foundation (178).
אֶשָּׁה*, אֶשָּׁא fire.
אָשַׁף enchanter (*53*, *188*).
אֻשַּׁרְנָא furnishings (?) (*189*).
אֶשְׁתַּדּוּר insurrection (*111*, 177, *190*).
אִשְׁתִּי* *see* שׁתה.
אָת* sign, miracle (92).
אתה to come; *hap̄.* (הַיְתִי) to bring (13, 15, 85, *124*, *148*, *151*, [*167*).
אַתּוּן furnace (*188*).
אֲתַר place, trace (?, *D 2:35*); אֲתַר דִּי there where; בָּאתַר *see* בָּאתַר (*52*, 84, *91*).

## ב

בְּ in, through, with (16, 27, 36, 62, *75*, 76, *77*, 80, 84, 86, 89, 90, 95, 177, 186).
בֵּאדַיִן *see* אֱדַיִן.

בְּאִישׁ* bad, evil (13, 15).

באשׁ (*ẹ/i*) to be evil, (בְּאֵשׁ עֲלוֹהִי) it grieved him (13, 82, *125*).

בָּאתַר, בָּתַר after (*prep.*) (13, *84*).

בָּבֶל Babylon (16, 26, 30, 48, 59).

בָּבְלָי* Babylonian (*58*).

בדר *pa.* to scatter (115).

בְּהִילוּ haste (*56*).

בהל *hitp.* to hurry; *pa.* to disturb; *hitpa.* to be disturbed (20, 88, *108*, 175).

בּוֹזְנַי *see* שְׁתַר בּוֹזְנַי.

בטל (*ẹ/i*) to be idle; *pa.* to cause to be idle, to stop someone from working (10, 23, *102*, 177).

בֵּין (*suff.* בֵּינֵיהֵון) between (*prep.*) (49, *84*).

בִּינָה discernment.

בִּירָה* fortress, (fortified) city (15, *188*).

בית to spend the night (*133*).

בַּיִת* (*pl. suff.* בָּתֵּיכוֹן) house (15, 17, 36, 46, 47, 48, *51*, *62*, 79, 80, 184).

בָּל mind (82).

בֵּלְאשַׁצַּר *see* בֵּלְשַׁאצַּר.

בלה *pa.* to wear out.

בְּלוֹ a kind of taxes, tribute (*188*).

בֵּלְטְשַׁאצַּר Belteshazzar (*13*, 36).

בֵּלְשַׁאצַּר Belshazzar (*13*).

בנה to build, to rebuild; *hitp.* to be built (rebuilt) (10, 36, 54, 79, 87, 111, *149*, *150*, 177).

בִּנְיָן* building (34).

בנס to become enraged.

בעה to search, to seek, to ask, to pray; *pa.* to search (17).

בָּעוּ request, prayer (*55*).

בְּעֵל master, (בְּעֵל טְעֵם) official in charge (10, 17, *51*, *188*).

בִּקְעָה* plain (*51*).

בקר *pa.* to search, to investigate; *hitpa.* to be searched, investigated (76).

בַּר (*pl.* בְּנִין*) son, (בַּר אֱלָהִין) a divine being, (בְּנֵי אֲנָשָׁא) human beings, (בְּנֵי תוֹרִין) young oxen (47, *62*, 74, 78, 80).

בַּר* (*det.* בָּרָא) field (186).
ברך to kneel *D 6:11.*
ברך *pa.* to bless (20, *115*).
בְּרַךְ* knee.
בְּרַם but (*85*).
בְּשַׂר flesh, mankind (*52*, 95, 96).
בַּת* (pl. בַּתִּין) bath (*liquid measure*).
בָּתַר *see* בָּאתַר.

## ג

גַּב* *see* גְּנַב*.
גֹּב (*det.* גֻּבָּא) den, pit (10, 20, 48, 78).
גְּבוּרָה* power (31).
גְּבַר (*pl.* גֻּבְרִין) man (30, 38, 48, *51*, 95, 184).
גִּבָּר* strong man (27).
גְּדָבַר* treasurer (17, *189*).
גדד to cut down (10, *160*).
גּוֹא (מִן ג׳, בְּג׳, לְג׳) midst, inside (*prep.*) (*5*, *84*).
גֵּוָה arrogance (10).
גוח *hap̄.* to stir up (*141*).
גִּזְבַּר (*pl. det.* גִּזַּבְרַיָּא) treasurer (17, *189*).
גזר *hitp.* to break off (*intrans.*) (104, *117*).
גָּזַר* exorcizer (*or some other kind of practitioner of super-natural craft*).
גְּזֵרָה* decision.
גִּיר* plaster, whitewash.
גַּלְגַּל* (*pl. suff.* גַּלְגִּלּוֹהִי) wheel (*of a chair*).
גלה to reveal; *hap̄.* to exile (10, *146*, 184).
גָּלוּ* exile (*55*, 80).
גְּלָל (אֶבֶן גְּלָל) hewn stone.
גְּמִיר completely (*88*).
גְּנַב* (*suff.* גַּבַּהּ) side.
גְּנַז* (*pl. det.* גִּנְזַיָּא) treasure (*189*).
גַּף* (*pl.* גַּפִּין) wing (*59*).
גְּרַם* bone.
גְּשֵׁם* body (*51*).

## ד

דְּ *see* דִּי.

דָּא this (*fem.*) (17, 30, *32*, *33*).

דֹּב bear.

דבח to sacrifice (17).

דְּבַח* sacrifice.

דבק to adhere.

דִּבְרַת (על [עד] דִּ׳ דִּי) so that (*86*).

דְּהַב gold (16, 17, 30, 46, *52*).

דֶּהָיֵא *read* דְּהוּא (*35*).

דור to dwell (12, 59, 87, *137*).

דּוּרָא Dura (*name of a locality*).

דוש to trample upon.

דַּחֲוָן table? (*other traditional guesses consider the word a pl. fem.:* concubines, food, musical instruments, perfume *D 6:19*).

דחל to fear, (דְּחִיל) frightful; *pa.* to frighten (40, 88).

דִּי *relative pronoun, subordinating conjunction* (16, 17, 30, *35—37*, 46, *48*, 62, 80, 83—85, *86*, 91, 95, 177, 184, 186).

דִּי לְ- *independent possessive pronoun* (*31*).

דִּי לָא without (*prep.*) (*84*, 87).

דִּי לְמָה lest (*86*).

דין to judge (*137*).

דִּין justice, court, law suit, judgment.

דַּיָּן* judge (40).

דִּינָיֵא *read* דַּיָּנַיָּא judges *E 4:9*.

דֵּךְ (*fem.* דָּךְ) that (*demonstrative pronoun*) (*32*, 87, 177).

דִּכֵּן that (*demonstrative pronoun*) (*32*).

דְּכַר* ram.

דִּכְרוֹן* memorandum (22).

דָּכְרָן* memorandum, (סְפַר דָּכְרָנַיָּא) record book (10, 17, 22, 27).

דלק to burn.

דמה to resemble.

דְּנָה this (16, 17, *32—34*, 47, 78, 82, 92, 96, 177, 184).

דָּנִיֵּאל Daniel (*13*, 30, 76, 77, 82, 89).

דקק to be crushed; *hap̄.* to crush (10, 104, 117, *158*, *164*).

דָּר generation (83).

דָּרְיָוֶשׁ Darius (< *OPers. Dārayavauš*) (26, 178).

דְּרָע* arm.

דָּת law, legal situation (30, *59*, 78, *189*).

דֶּתֶא* vegetation, grass (186).

דְּתָבַר* law official (16, *189*).

## ה

הֲ, הַ *introducing questions* (30, 93, *94*, 95).

הָא behold (*91*).

הֵא כְדִי as (*conj.*) (*86*).

הַדָּבַר* companion (*189*).

הַדָּם* limb (*189*).

הדר *pa.* to glorify.

הֲדַר* glory.

הוּא he, that (*demonstrative pronoun*) (13, *29*, *30*, *32*, 33, *34*, 35).

הוה to be (10, 79, *132*, *145*, *147*, *148*, *168*, *177*).

הוך to go (*134*, *136*, *169*, 178).

הִיא she (13, *29*, *30*, 31).

הֵיכַל palace, temple (*188*).

הֵימַן *see* אמן.

הַיְתִי *see* אתה.

הלך *pa.*, *hap̄.* to walk about (*169*).

הֲלָךְ a kind of taxes (85, *188*).

הִמּוֹ they, them (26, *29*, *30*, 84, 174, 184).

הִמּוֹן them (*29*, 174, 184).

המונך* (*det. qᵊrē* הַמְנִיכָא, correctly *הַמְיָנֵךְ) necklace (*189*).

הֵן if, (הֵן ··· הֵן) either . . . or (*86*, 95).

הַצְדָּא really? (*93*).

הַרְהֹר* (*pl.*) imaginings (39).

## ו

וְ and (27, 30, 46, 47, 63, 74, 76, 78, 81, 83, 84, *85*, 86, 89, 177—179, 181, 184).

## ז

זבן to buy.
זְהִיר* warned, careful (*not to do something*).
זוד *see* זיד.
זון *hitp.* to obtain food, to feed (*138*).
זוע to tremble (17).
זיד (זוד) *hap̄.* to act impiously (*142*).
זִיו* facial features, radiant healthy complexion, splendor (10, *188*).
זָכוּ innocence (*18*, *188*).
זְכַרְיָה Zechariah.
זמן *hitp.* to agree upon (*114*).
זְמַן time, (בֵּהּ זִמְנָא) at the very time, moment (*52*, *89*).
זְמָר* music (46).
זַמָּר* musician (40).
זַן* kind, species (46, *189*).
זְעֵיר* small.
זעק (*ẹ/i*) to shout, to call.
זְקִיף crucified.
זְרֻבָּבֶל Zerubbabel.
זְרַע seed, semen.

## ח

חֲבוּלָה harm, damage.
חבל *pa.* to harm, to damage, to destroy; *hitpa.* to be destroyed.
חֲבָל damage, harm.
חֲבַר* colleague (*52*).
חַבְרָה* (*fem.*) colleague, counterpart (80).
חַגַּי Haggai.
חַד one (30, *46*, *63*, *64*, *70*, 78, 80, 82). *See also* כַּחֲדָה.
חֲדֵה* breast (*54*).
חֶדְוָה joy (*55*).
חֲדַת new.
חוה *pa.*, *hap̄.* to tell, to inform someone about something (10, *111*, *132*, *147*, *153*, *176*).
20 חוט, חיט *see* יחט.

חִוָּר white.
חזה to see, (חֲזֵה) seeming, appropriate, usual (91, *116*).
חֲזוּ* vision, appearance (*55*, 80, 83).
חֲזוּת* appearance (*55*).
חטא *pa.* to make a sin-offering (*187*).
חֲטָא* sin (*14*).
חַי (*det.* חַיָּא) living, alive, living being (30, 80).
חיה to live; *hap̄.* to let live, to keep alive (43, 79, *148*, *170*).
חַיְוָה animal, animals (15, 34, *49*, 83, 184).
חַיִּן life (79).
חַ֫יִל strength, might, force, army, (בְּחַ֫יִל) aloud (25, 27, *51*).
חַכִּים wise, sage (40).
חָכְמָה wisdom (16, 31, *51*, 80, 84, 95).
חֵ֫לֶם dream (34, *51*).
חלף to pass by.
חֲלָק share, tax revenue.
חֲמָה, חֵמָה wrath.
חֲמַר wine (46, *51*).
חִנְטָה* (*pl.* חִנְטִין) wheat (*61*).
חֲנֻכָּה* inauguration.
חנן to show mercy; *hiṯpa.* to seek mercy (*161*).
חֲנַנְיָה Hananiah.
חַסִּיר wanting, deficient.
חסן *hap̄.* to possess, to take possession of (*116*).
חֲסַן* (det. חִסְנָא) power.
חֲסַף clay, earthenware.
חצף *hap̄. part. pass.* urgent (*116*).
חרב *hap̄.* to destroy (10, *116*).
חַרְטֹם (*pl. det.* חַרְטֻמַּיָּא) magician (*23*, *187*).
חרך *hiṯpa.* to be scorched.
*21* חֲרַץ* (*suff.* חַרְצֵהּ) hip, loins.
חשׁב to consider (87).
חֲשׁוֹךְ* darkness.
חֲשַׁח* needed, needing (*44*, *188*).
חַשְׁחוּ* needs (*56*).
חשׁל to smash.
חתם to seal.

## ט

טאב (*ẹ/i*) to be good, (טְאֵב עֲלוֹהִי) it pleased him (82, *125*, 128).
טָב good (17, 22, *42*, 128).
טַבָּח* butcher, executioner (17, 40).
טוּר mountain (17, 79).
טְוָת fasting (*adv.*) (*88*).
טִין* clay.
טַל dew (17, 76).
טלל *hap̄.* to seek shade (shelter) (17, *157*).
טעם *pa.* to feed (*trans.*) (181).
טְעֵם, טַעַם order, decree, information, attention, influence (*of wine*) (*51*, 80, 178, *188*). *See also* בְּעֵל.
טְפַר* fingernail, claw (17).
טרד to drive out (181).
טַרְפְּלָיֵא *meaning?* (*191*).

## י

יבל *hap̄.* (הֵיבֵל) to bring (*130*). *See also* סובל.
יַבֶּשָׁה* (*det.* יַבֶּשְׁתָּא) dry land.
יְגַר heap of stones.
יַד hand (10, 17, 25, 26, 36, *45*, *59*, *84*).
ידה *hap̄.* to laud (*130*).
ידע to know; *hap̄.* to let know (10, 17, 21, 26, 88, 111, 117, *128—130*, 174, 175, 177).
יהב to give, to lay (*foundations*); *hitp.* to be given (36, 80, 84, 118, *129*, 179).
יְהוּד Judaea (76).
יְהוּדָי* Jew, Jewish (42, *58*, 83, 95).
יוֹם (*pl.* יוֹמִין, *יוֹמָן) day (*62*, *74*, 80, 81, 177).
יוֹצָדָק Jozadak.
(?) יחט *pa.* to lay (*foundations?*) (*178*).
יטב to be good, it pleases (*128*).
יכל (*ẹ/i*) to be able, to prevail (*128*, *171*).
יַם* (*det.* יַמָּא) sea.
יסף *hap̄.* to add (27, *130*).
יעט *hitpa.* to take counsel with each other, to agree after mutual consultation.

| | |
|---|---|
| יָעֵט* | adviser (17, 66). |
| יצב | *pa.* to make certain. |
| יַצִּיב | certain, (יַצִּיבָא) certainly (*88*). |
| יָקֵד* | fiery, burning. |
| יְקֵדָה* | burning, conflagration (10). |
| יַקִּיר* | important, difficult. |
| יְקָר | (יְקַר? *D 4:33*) honor. |
| יְרוּשְׁלֶם | Jerusalem (76, 84). |
| יְרַח | month (*74*). |
| יְרַךְ* | (*יַרְכָה?, *pl. suff.* יַרְכָתֵהּ) thigh (*51*). |
| יִשְׂרָאֵל | Israel (47, 75, 80, 187). |
| יֵשׁוּעַ | Jeshua. |
| יָת* | *prep. introducing the direct object* (*31*, *84*). |
| יתב | (*ẹ/i*) to sit, to be settled; *hap̄.* to settle (trans.) (10, 17, *128*, *130*). |
| יַתִּיר | excessive, (יַתִּירָא, יַתִּירָא) excessively (*88*). |

## כ

| | |
|---|---|
| כְּ | like as, comparable to, according to (16, 33, 74, *75*, *78*, 84, 87, 92, 149, 181). *See also* כְּדִי, כַּחֲדָה, כְּעַן, כְּעֶת, כְּעֶנֶת. |
| כְּדַב* | (fem. כְּדָבָה) untrue (15). |
| כְּדִי | when (78, *86*). *See also* הֵא כְדִי. |
| כָּה | here (81, *91*). |
| כהל | (*ẹ/i?*) to be able (95, *171*). |
| כָּהֵן* | priest (*187*). |
| כַּוָּה* | (*pl.* כַּוִּין) window (*61*). |
| כּוֹרֶשׁ | Cyrus (< *OPers. Kūruš*) (26). |
| כַּחֲדָה | together, without distinction (*64*, *93*). |
| כַּכַּר* | talent (*monetary unit*) (81). |
| כֹּל | (כָּל, כֹּלָּא) totality, every, entire, all (10, 26, 36, 46, 47, 49, 80, 84, 85, 87, 88, *96*). |
| כָּל קֳבֵל | *see* קֳבֵל. |
| כלל | *see* שׁכלל. |
| כְּמָה | how! (*92*). |
| כֵּן | thus (*92*). |
| כְּנָה* | (*כְּנָת?) colleague (*62*, *188*). |

כְּנֵמָא thus (26, *92*).
כנשׁ to assemble (*trans.*); *hitpa.* to assemble (*intrans.*) (177).
כַּסְדָּי* *see* כַּשְׂדָּי.
כְּסַף silver (46, *51*, 81).
כְּעַן (כְּעֶנֶת ,כְּעֶת) now, now then (*89*, 183).
כפת to bind; *pa.* to bind (10).
כֹּר* kor (*solid measure*).
כַּרְבְּלָה* hat (*189*).
כרה *hitp.* to become sick, sad (*151*).
כָּרוֹז* herald (40, 177).
כרז* *hap̄.* to announce publicly.
כָּרְסֵא (*pl.* כָּרְסָוָן) chair, throne (10, *54*, *188*).
כַּשְׂדָּי (כַּסְ׳) Chaldaean (14, 19, *58*).
כתב to write (17, 23, 26, *101*, *105*, *110*, *111*, 177).
כְּתָב writing, text, document, letter, stipulation in writing (78).
כְּתַל (*pl. det.* כֻּתְלַיָּא) wall (*of a house*) (*51*).

## ל

לְ to, for (5, 10, 27, 31, 33, 36, 43, *47*, 49, 74, *75*, 76, 78, *79*, 84—86, 111, 118, 171, 177—179, 181, *182*, 187).
לָא not, (לָה) nought (30, 59, 77, 85, 86, *87*, 94, 95). *See also* דִּי לָא.
לֵב* (*suff.* לִבִּי) heart.
לְבַב heart (83).
לְבוּשׁ* garment (10).
לבשׁ to be dressed, to wear; *hap̄.* to dress (*trans.*) (10).
לָה *see* לָא.
לֶהֱוֵא (לֶהֶוְיָן ,לֶהֱוֹן) *see* הוה (*168*).
לָהֵן but, except (*85*).
לֵוָי* Levite (*187*).
לְוָת* with, at (*chez*) (*84*).
לְחֶם meal, banquet (*51*).
לְחֵנָה* maid servant (10).
לֵילֵא* (*det.* לֵילְיָא) night (*54*, 83, 89).
לְמָה lest (*86*, 87). *See also* דִּי לְמָה.
לְקֳבֵל *see* קֳבֵל.
לִשָּׁן* tongue, language.

# מ

מֵ-, מִ- *see* מִן.
מְאָה hundred (*63*, 81).
מֹאזְנַיָה (מֹאזַנְיָה) (*pl. det.*) scales (13).
מָאן* vessel (13, 34, 46, 184).
מָאתַ֫יִן two hundred (13, *45*, *63*).
מְגִלָּה scroll (46).
מגר *pa.* to overthrow.
מַדְבַּח* altar (17).
מִדָּה *see* מִנְדָּה.
מְדוֹר* (?מָדוֹר*) dwelling (22).
מָדַי Media (< *OPers. Māda, through Akk. Madai*) (78).
מָדָי* Median.
מְדִינָה* province (10, 15, 48).
מְדָר dwelling (22, 95).
מָה what?, whatever (*37*, *38*). *See also* כְּמָה.
מוֹת death (86).
מָזוֹן food (17, 23).
מחא to hit; *pa.* to hit, (יְמַחֵא בִידֵהּ) to stay (His hand); *hitp.* to be beaten, to be affixed (17).
מַחְלְקָה* division, group.
מטא, מטה to come, to go (*76*, 81).
מִישָׁאֵל Mishael.
מֵישַׁךְ Meshach.
מלא to fill; *hitp.* to be filled.
מַלְאַךְ* angel (*187*).
מִלָּה (*pl.* מִלִּין) word, speech, matter (33, 47, *61*, 84, 86, 90).
מלח to partake of salt.
מְלַח salt (*51*).
מֶ֫לֶךְ king (15, 32, 36, 40, 42, 43, 47, *51*, 62, 79, 80, 82—84, 88, 90, 99, 111, 177, *189*).
מְלֵךְ* (*suff.* מִלְכִּי) advice (*51*).
מַלְכָּה* queen (*51*).
מַלְכוּ kingdom, reign (36, 40, 47, *56*, 74, 79, 84, 89, 179).
מלל *pa.* to speak (10, 24, 83, 84).
מַן who?, (מַן דִּי) whoever (30, *37*, *38*).

מִן (מִ-) from (17, 20, 33, 64, *75*, 76, *80*, 81, 84—86, 88, 89, 91, 177, 181).
מִן דִּי as soon as, after (*conj.*) (*86*).
מְנֵא mina (*monetary unit*) (*188*).
מִנְדָּה, מִדָּה a kind of taxes (*188*).
מַנְדַּע knowledge (21, 82, 128).
מנה to count, to number; *pa.* to appoint (26, *153*).
מִנְחָה (sacrificial) offering (*187*).
מִנְיָן number.
מַעְבָד* work, deed (10, 36).
מְעֵה* belly (*54*).
מֶעָל* entrance, (מֶעָלֵי שִׁמְשָׁא) sunset (159).
מָרֵא lord, master (13, *54*, *62*).
מְרַד rebellion (177).
מָרָד* rebellious (15).
מרט to pluck out, to tear off.
מֹשֶׁה Moses (78).
מְשַׁח oil.
מִשְׁכַּב* bed.
מִשְׁכַּן* dwelling.
מַשְׁרוֹקִי* pipe (*musical instr.*) (46, *57*).
מִשְׁתֵּא* banquet (40).
מַתְּנָה* gift (17).

## נ

נבא *hitpa.* to prophesy.
נְבוּאָה* prophecy, prophetical office (187).
נְבוּכַדְנֶצַּר Nebuchadnezzar (*Akk. Nābu-kudurrī-uṣur*) (84).
נְבִזְבָּה (*pl. suff.* נְבִזְבְּיָתָךְ) gift (*62*, *190*).
נְבִיא* prophet (*187*).
נֶבְרְשָׁה* (*det.* נֶבְרַשְׁתָּא) lamp (*190*).
נגד to flow.
נֶגֶד toward (*84*).
נְגַהּ* (*det.* נָגְהָא) dawn (*51*, 186).
נְגוֹ *see* עֲבֵד נְגוֹ.
נדב *hitpa.* to volunteer, to contribute voluntarily (111).
נִדְבָּךְ layer (*of a building*) (*188*).

נדד to flee (*158*).

*נְדַן (נִדְנֶה, *read* נִדְנַהּ) container, sheath (10, *190*).

*נְהוֹר (*det. k*ᵊ*ṯīḇ* נהירא, *q*ᵊ*rē* נְהוֹרָא) light.

נַהִירוּ brilliance (*56*).

נְהַר river (188).

נוד to flee.

נְוָלוּ, נְוָלִי dunghill (*57*, *190*).

נוּר fire (*59*, 184).

נזק to suffer harm, to suffer damage; *hap̄.* to harm, to cause damage to (99, *111*).

נְחָשׁ copper.

נחת to go down, to descend; *hap̄.* to bring down, to deposit (184).

נטל to lift up (178).

נטר to guard (17).

נִיחוֹחִין sacrifices of sweet smell (*187*).

*נְכַס (*pl.* נִכְסִין) possessions, property (47, 86, *188*).

נְמַר panther.

נסח *hiṯp.* to be torn out.

נסך *pa.* to pour out (*libations*).

נְסַךְ (*pl. suff.* נִסְכֵּיהוֹן) libation (*51*, *187*).

נפל to fall, to be necessary (10, 12, *118*).

נפק to go out, to come out; *hap̄.* to take out, to bring out (*119*, 177).

*נִפְקָה expenses (80).

*נִצְבָּה seed, planting, mineral (*traditional:* strength) (80).

נצח *hiṯpa.* to distinguish oneself (82).

נצל *hap̄.* to save.

נְקֵא clean, pure, lamb.

נקשׁ to knock.

נשׂא to lift up, to take, to carry; *hiṯpa.* to rise up (82, *118*, *119*, *126*, 177, 184).

*נְשִׁין (*suff.* נְשֵׁיהוֹן) *see* אַנְתָּה.

*נִשְׁמָה breath, soul (36, 84).

נְשַׁר eagle.

*נִשְׁתְּוָן written order (*189*).

*נְתִין temple servant (*187*).

נתן to give (*118*, 129, 175).

נתר *hap̄.* to shake off (*115*).

## ס

סַבְּךְ* *see* *שַׂבְּךְ.
סבר to hope, to intend (19).
סגד (*ẹ/i*) to prostrate oneself (*102, 106*).
סְגַן* (*pl.* סִגְנִין) prefect (*188*).
סגר to lock (10, 85).
*22* סובל *part. pass.* (מְסוֹבְלִין) laid (*foundations*) (*130*, 166, *188*).
סוּמְפֹּנְיָה (סיפניה) symphony (bagpipe*?*) (*46, 191*).
סוף to end, to cease; *hap̄.* to make an end to (26, *141*).
סוֹף end.
סיפניה *see* סוּמְפֹּנְיָה.
סלק (*ẹ/i*) to go up, to come up; *hap̄.* to bring up (21, 23, *172*).
סעד *pa.* to help (20).
סְפַר book, document (27, *51*, 78).
סָפַר* scribe, secretary.
סַרְבָּל* trousers (*189*).
סָרַךְ* chief minister (82, *189*).
סתר *pa.* to conceal (*44*).
סתר to tear down (19, 184).

## ע

עבד to do, to make; *hitp̱.* to be made, to be done (10, 27, 83, *116*, 177, 189).
עֲבֵד servant, slave (29, 30, *51*).
עֲבֵד נְגוֹ Abed-nego.
עֲבִידָה* work, administration, service, worship (15, 17, 48).
עֲבַר נַהֲרָא across-the-River, Trans-Euphrates Province (Syria) (*188*).
עַד until (*prep.*) (75, 76, *81*, 89). *See also* דִּבְרַת.
עַד, עַד דִּי until (*conj.*) (*86, 178*).
עדה to come forth, to pass away, to become invalid; *hap̄.* to remove (59, *76*, *116*, 184).
עִדּוֹא Iddo (*5*).
עִדָּן time, season (year) (*66*, 86).
עוֹד still, yet (*90*).
עֲוָיָה iniquity, misdeed.
עוֹף bird, birds.

עוּר chaff.
עֵז* (*pl.* עִזִּין) goat (*59*).
עִזְקָה* seal ring.
עֶזְרָא Ezra.
עֲזַרְיָה Azariah.
עֵטָה advice, counsel (10, 17, 129).
עַ֫יִן* eye (*51*, *59*, 178).
עִיר a kind of angel.
עַל upon (10, 26, 33, 49, 75, 76, *82*, 84, 86, 177, 178).
עֵ֫לָּא above (*adv.*) (80, *88*).
עִלָּה cause, pretext.
עֲלָוָה* sacrifice (79).
עִלָּי* most high (84).
עִלִּי* (*suff.* עִלִּיתֵהּ) upper room (*57*).
עֶלְיוֹן* most high (*22*, 179, 187).
עלל to enter; *hap̄.* to let enter (17, 20, 26, *76*, *158*, *162*, *164*, [175).
עָלַם eternity (43, *53*, 62, 79, 80, 177).
עֵלְמָי* Elamite.
עֲלַע* (*pl.* עִלְעִין) rib (17, *59*).
עַם (*det.* עַמָּא, *pl.* עַמְמַיָּא) people (17, 20, *62*, 179, 184).
עִם (together) with (75, 76, *83*, 95).
עַמִּיק* deep (*44*).
עֲמַר wool (17).
עֵ֫ן* (*עֶנֶת, *עֶת) *see* כְּעַן, *etc.*
ענה to answer (*150*).
עֲנֵה* humble, poor (*25*).
עֲנָן* cloud.
עֲנַף* branch (*of a tree*).
עֲנָשׁ fine (*punishment*) (47, 86).
עֳפִי* (*suff.* עָפְיַהּ) foliage (*51*).
עֲצִיב sad.
עקר *hitp.* to be uprooted (*115*).
עִקַּר (עִקָּר) offshoot.
עַר* (עָרַר?, *pl. suff.* עָרָיךְ) adversary (17).
ערב *pa.* to mix (*trans.*); *hitpa.* to mix (*intrans.*) (*76*).
עֲרָד* onager, wild ass.
עַרְוָה* nakedness, shame.
עֲשַׂב vegetation, grass (75, 181, 186).

עֲשַׂר ten (45, *63*).

עֶשְׂרִין twenty (*63*).

עֲשִׁית concerned about.

*עֲתִיד ready, prepared (95).

עַתִּיק old (81).

## פ

פֶּחָה (*pl.* *פַּחֲוָן) governor (36, *62*, *188*).

פֶּחָר potter.

*פַּטִּישׁ shirt (*?*) (*189*).

פלג to divide.

פְּלַג half (*71*).

*פְּלֻגָּה section, group.

פלח to serve, to worship (36, 85, 95, *115*).

פָּלְחָן service, worship, cult (10).

פֻּם (*suff.* פֻּמֵּהּ) mouth (20, 90).

פַּס palm (of a hand, *or some other* part of a hand).

פְּסַנְתֵּרִין (פְּסַנְטֵ׳) psaltery (16, *46*, *191*).

פַּרְזֶל iron (39, *188*).

פרס to divide.

פְּרֵס half-mina (*or* half-shekel) (*monetary unit*) (*188*).

פָּרַס Persia (< *OPers. Pārsa*).

*פָּרְסָי Persian.

פרק to atone for, redeem.

פרשׁ *pa.* to interpret.

פַּרְשֶׁגֶן copy (*51*, *189*).

פשׁר to interpret; *pa.* (*?*) to interpret (*111*).

פְּשַׁר interpretation (*51*).

פִּתְגָם message, word, matter (*15*, *189*).

פתח to open (61).

*פְּתָי breadth (*54*).

## צ

צבה (*ẹ/i*) to want, to wish (17, *145*, *149*).

צְבוּ thing, matter (*55*, 77).

צבע *pa.* to wet; *hiṭpa.* to be wetted (*76*, *114*).

צד side (*84*).
צְדָא* *see* הַצְדָא.
צִדְקָה charity.
צַוַּאר* neck (*13*).
צלה *pa.* to pray (79).
צלח *hap̄.* to make successful, to prosper (*intrans.*), to succeed (17, *111*).
צְלֵם, צֶלֶם image, statue, complexion (17, 32, 34, 46, *51*).
צְפִיר* (צְפִירֵי עִזִּין) he-goat.
צִפַּר* bird (10, *59*).

## ק

קבל *pa.* to receive, to take over.
קֳבֵל (כָּל קֳבֵל, לְקֳבֵל) facing, opposite, corresponding to (*prep.*), (כָּל קֳבֵל דִּי) because (*conj.*) (10, 33, *84*, *86*, 96, 177).
קַדִּישׁ* holy, saint (83, 179).
קֳדָם before (*prep.*) (*10*, 25, 80, *84*, 85).
קַדְמָי* first (*69*).
קַדְמַת (מִקַּ׳, מִן קַ׳) before (*prep.*) (*84*, 177).
קום to stand, to arise, to last; *pa.* to establish; *hap̄.* to set up, to install, to appoint, to issue (*an interdict*) (14, 23, 117, *133—137*, *139—142*, 177).
קטל to kill; *pa.* to kill; *hitp.*, *hitpa.* to be killed (184).
קְטַר* (*pl.* קִטְרִין) knot, joint, difficult problem.
קַיִט summer (17, 26, *51*).
קְיָם statute.
קַיָּם enduring.
קִיתְרוֹס (*qᵊrē* קַתְ׳) zither (*46*, *191*).
קָל sound, voice (46).
קנה to purchase.
קצף to become angry (88).
קְצַף wrath.
קצץ *pa.* to cut off.
קְצָת end, part (80, *84*).
קרא to call, to call out, to read aloud, to read; *hitp.* to be called (10, *108*, *146*, *152*, 177).

קרב (ẹ/*i*) to draw near, to approach; *pa.* to offer (*sacrifices*); *hap̄.* to bring near, to offer (*sacrifices*) (10, 26, 78).
קְרָב war (83, *188*).
קִרְיָה* (*pl. det.* קִרְיָה) city (*62*, 87, 177).
קֶרֶן horn (*of animals, musical instrument*) (*45*, 46, *51*, *59*).
קְרַץ* piece, (*אכל קַרְצִין) to denounce, to slander (cf. Akk.).
קְשֹׁט truth (10, 36, *51*, 80, 86).

## ר

רֵאשׁ head, chief (13, 17, 30, *62*).
רַב (*det.* רַבָּא, *pl.* רַבְרְבִין) great, big, (*pl.* *רַבְרְבָנִין) chief, magnate (*44*, 47, 59, 61, *62*, 80, 92).
רבה to grow; *pa.* to make someone a magnate (*145*).
רְבוּ greatness (*55*).
רִבּוֹ (*pl. kᵊṯīḇ* רבון) myriad (*62*, *63*).
רְבִיעָי* fourth (*69*).
רגז *hap̄.* to anger.
רְגַז anger (*51*).
רְגַל* foot (*45*, *59*).
23 רגשׁ *hap̄.* to assemble (*intrans.*).
רֵו* appearance.
רוּחַ wind, spirit (*59*).
רום (ẹ/*i*) to be high, to be haughty; *hap̄.* to raise up; *רוֹמֵם to exalt; *הִתְרוֹמַם to exalt oneself (23, *133*, *141*, *143*, 157).
רוּם* height.
רָז secret, mystery (16, 82, *189*).
רְחוּם Rehum.
רַחִיק* remote.
רַחֲמִין mercy.
רחץ *hitp.* to trust.
רֵיחַ smell (*59*).
רמה to throw, to set up (*chairs*), to impose (*taxes*); *hitp.* to be thrown.
רְעוּ* wish, pleasure (17, *55*).
רַעְיוֹן* thought (22).

רַעְנַן relaxed.
רעע to break; *pa.* to break, to crush (20, *159*).
רפס to trample upon.
רשם to draw, to draw up, to inscribe, to write.

## שׂ

שָׂב* elder (83).
שַׂבְּךְ* ('סַ) sambuke (harp) (19, 46).
שׂגא to be (become) much (great).
שַׂגִּיא much, many, great, (*adv.*) much, greatly, very (13, 61, *88*, 177).
שָׂהֲדוּ* testimony (*56*).
שְׂטַר side (46).
שׂים to place, to set, to appoint, to give (*an order, a name*), to pay (*attention*); *hitp.* to be placed, to be made, to be given (*order*) (36, 80, 82, 117, *133—136, 138*).
שׂכל *hitpa.* to observe (*114*).
שָׂכְלְתָנוּ intelligence (*56*).
שָׂנֵא* enemy (13, *126*).
שְׂעַר hair.

## שׁ

שׁאל (*ẹ/i*) to ask (17, 24, 26, *125*, 175).
שְׁאֵלָה* question, problem (15).
שְׁאַלְתִּיאֵל Shealtiel.
שְׁאָר rest, remnant (184).
שׁבח *pa.* to praise (24, *115*, *117*).
שְׁבַט* tribe (*187*).
שְׁבִיב* flame (184).
שְׁבַע* seven (*63*, *66*, *70*, 82).
שׁבק to leave; *hitp.* to be left (26, *114*).
שׁבשׁ *hitpa.* to be confused (*114*).
שֵׁגְלָה* concubine (*188*).
שׁדר *hitpa.* to make efforts (111).
שַׁדְרַךְ Shadrach.
שׁוה *pa.* to make equal, to place; *hitpa.* to be made (83, *132*).

שׁוּר* wall (*of a city*) (178).

שׁוּשַׁנְכָי* man from Susa (< *OPers.* **Šūšanaka*).

שְׁחִית corrupt, (*fem.*) fault, corruption (*44*).

שׁיזב to save (10, 49, 84, *166*, 175, *188*).

שׁיצי(א) to complete (*18*, *166*, *188*).

שׁכח *hitp.* to be found; *hap̄.* to find (26, *114*, *115*, *117*).

שׁכלל to complete; *hištap̄ʿal* to be completed (*157*, 166, 178, *188*).

שׁכן to dwell; *pa.* to cause to dwell.

שְׁלֵה happy, carefree.

24 שָׁלוּ, שָׁלָה negligence (*55*).

שְׁלֵוָה* happiness.

שׁלח to send, to send a message (*by messenger*, *letter*) (82).

שׁלט (*ẹ/i*) to rule, to have power over, to overpower; *hap̄.* to give power to (*76*, *102*, *110*).

שִׁלְטֹן* authority, official (22).

שָׁלְטָן rule, domination, dominion (22, 184).

שַׁלִּיט (*adj.*) mighty, powerful, being in control, authorized, (*noun*) (*powerful*) official (10, 17, 40).

שׁלם (*ẹ/i*) to be completed; *hap̄.* to finish, to bring to an end, to hand over (*102*).

שְׁלָם well-being, greetings (96).

שֻׁם (*pl.* *שְׁמָהָן) name (30, 36, 38, 48, *62*).

שׁמד *hap̄.* to exterminate.

25 שְׁמַיִן* (*det.* שְׁמַיָּא) heaven (17, 36, 47, 59, 75, 84, 178).

שׁמם (אֶשְׁתּוֹמַם) to be perturbed (*157*).

שׁמע to hear; *hitpa.* to obey (17).

שָׁמְרַיִן* (*pausal* שָׁמְרָיִן) Samaria (25, 62).

שׁמשׁ *pa.* to serve.

שְׁמַשׁ* (*det.* שִׁמְשָׁא) sun (*51*).

שִׁמְשַׁי Shimshai.

שֵׁן* (dual שִׁנַּיִן) tooth (*45*, *59*).

שׁנה to be different, to change (*intrans.*); *pa.* to cause a change, to change (*trans.*), to distinguish; *hitpa.* to change (*intrans.*); *hap̄.* to change (*trans.*) (*77*, *108*, *150*, *152*).

שְׁנָה* (*pl.* שְׁנִין) year (30, *61*, *74*, 78, 177).

שֵׁנָה* (*suff.* שִׁנְתֵּהּ) sleep (129).

שָׁעָה hour, while, (בַּהּ שַׁעֲתָא) at this very hour, moment (46, *62*, 78, *89*, 177).

שָׁפֵט* judge (*18*, 187).

שַׁפִּיר beautiful.

שפל *hap̄.* to bring down, to humiliate, to humble (10).

שְׁפַל low.

שפר to be good, it pleases.

שְׁפַרְפָּר* dawn (39, 186).

שָׁק* leg.

שרה to loosen, to unfetter, to explain (*knotty problems*), to reside (שְׁרֵה residing); *pa.* to solve (*?*), to begin; *hiṯpa.* to be loosened (*111*, *150*).

שְׁרֹשׁ* (*pl. suff.* שָׁרְשׁוֹהִי) root (*51*).

שרשו (*qᵉrē* שְׁרֹשִׁי) corporal punishment (19, *57*, 86, *189*).

שֵׁשְׁבַּצַּר Sheshbazzar (= שנאבצר* ?, *Akk. Sin-ab-uṣur*).

שֵׁת, שִׁת six (*63*, 74).

שתה (*ẹ/i*, אִשְׁתִּי*) to drink (46, *77*, *145*, *150*, *173*).

שִׁתִּין sixty (*63*, 74, 78).

שְׁתַר בּוֹזְנַי Shethar-bozenai (= שתברזן, < *OPers. Šatibṛjāna* "desiring joy").

## ת

תְּבִיר* fragile.

תְּדִיר* (בִּתְדִירָא) constantly.

תוב to return (*intrans.*); *hap̄.* to return (*trans.*) (82, *141*, *142*, 178, 184).

תוה to be perturbed (*132*).

תּוֹר* ox (17, 181).

תְּחוֹת, תְּחֹת* underneath (*prep.*) (22, 47, *84*).

תְּלַג snow (*51*).

תְּלִיתָי* third (14, *69*).

תְּלַת* (*det.* תַּלְתָּא) triumvir (*71*, *188*).

תְּלָת three, (תְּלָתְהוֹן) the three of them (17, 22, 23, 59, *63*, *66*, *73*, 74).

תְּלָתִין thirty (*63*, 81).

תַּמָּה there (17, *91*).

תְּמַהּ* wonder (92).

תִּנְיָן* second (69).
תִּנְיָנוּת again (*72*, *88*).
תִּפַּת* (*pl. det.* תִּפְתָּיֵא) police chief (*58*, *189*).
תַּקִּיף* strong, powerful (*88*, 92).
תקל to weigh.
תְּקֵל shekel (*monetary unit*).
תקן *hap̄.* to restore.
תקף (*ẹ*/*i*) to be (become) strong; *pa.* to strengthen, to issue a strong (*prohibition*) (*102*).
תְּקָף (*det.* תָּקְפָּא) strength (*10*, *51*).
תְּרֵין* (*fem.* תַּרְתֵּין) two (*45*, *63*, *65*, 74, 78).
תְּרַע door, gate, (royal) court (17).
תָּרָע* doorkeeper (20, 40).
תַּרְתֵּין *see* * תְּרֵין.
תַּתְּנַי Tattenai (*Akk. Tattannai*).